The Assistant Principals' Path to Promotion

The Assistant Principals' Path to Promotion

12 Power Plays to Develop a Winning Mindset, Lead with Impact, and Get Student Results

_____

Dr. Bobbie Mills

ISBN: 979-8-218-82092-3

Printed in the United States of America   1 2 2 9 2 5

♾This paper meets the requirements of ANSI/NISO Z39.48-1992 (Permanence of Paper)

Cover Design: Justin W. Hardin of Demascus Media
Photo: Charisma Howard of A Brew & You Photography
Editors: Dr. Joel Boyce of JCBEDPRO and Madeleine Stewart

For more information, please visit:
www.getelevatedvision.com

This book is for the principal inside you. Your promotion is coming. You are the leader your school has been waiting for. Rise and make your impact.

CONTENTS

VOICES FROM THE PATH INSTRUCTIONAL LEADERSHIP INTERVIEW

INTRODUCTION

Welcome to *The Assistant Principal's Path to Promotion: 12 Power Plays to Develop a Winning Mindset, Lead with Impact, and Get Student Results*. My hope is that by the time you reach the end of this book, you will have shifted your mindset to think and lead like a principal, built a practical leadership toolkit you can rely on, and gained the confidence and visibility needed to step into a principalship with readiness and impact.

If you are reading this book, then I know you are an assistant principal who wants to do more than just manage discipline and logistics. However, you have been struggling to balance the demands of being second in command while trying to grow into the leader you want to become.

You've been running on a hamster wheel, handling student discipline and putting out daily fires while trying to prove you are ready for the next level of leadership. I know that weight because I carried it also when I served as an assistant principal. You're constantly called to deal with the same handful of students, stepping into classrooms only when there are issues, and getting pulled into situations that consume your day before it starts. You feel like you are managing chaos instead of making an impact. You wonder if anyone sees you as more than just the assistant principal who handles problems.

You may feel like there is no clear path to become a principal. You are working hard and doing everything asked of you, yet no one has shown you what it actually takes to transition from assistant principal-ship to the principalship. You get feedback, but it doesn't always translate into concrete steps that prepare you for a principalship. You feel like you're waiting on someone to finally say you're ready, but time and time again, you witness others being promoted over you.

Maybe you feel undervalued. You spend endless hours managing crises and keeping the school afloat, yet your dedication often goes unnoticed. Over time, the weight of being overlooked drains you spiritually, mentally, and physically, leaving you stuck in a cycle you know you must break if you're ever going to find a clear path to the principalship.

I wrote this book to remind you that you are more than a disciplinarian or task manager. You are a leader in the making. Every challenge you face is an opportunity to sharpen your skills, expand your impact, and step closer to the principalship you are preparing for.

I've spent over two decades in education, serving as a classroom teacher, assistant principal, principal, and district level director. Along the way I was honored to be named Principal of the Year, but one of my proudest accomplishments occurred in my very first year as principal when I helped move my school from a D to a C.

I've had the privilege of coaching and advising many assistant principals on how to carve their own path to the principalship, but my journey wasn't always smooth, and the lessons I learned the hard way are the same lessons I now share with others to help them move forward with clarity and confidence.

I became an assistant principal after having taught English language arts for nine years at one of the largest middle schools in the district where I worked. I had just graduated from college with a master's degree in school administration. Little did I know that taking all those courses had not prepared me for what I actually signed up for. Once I became an assistant principal, let's just say I was baptized by fire. Unfortunately, I had inherited the discipline role, leaving me with few opportunities to be exposed to strategic, instructional, and cultural leadership, which I knew were essential for me to move up to a principalship.

I spent 11 years across two Title I schools. Every day, I found myself inundated with discipline. Mornings often started with a stack of 10 to 20 referrals left in my mailbox or slid underneath my door. I realized that handling discipline was a part of my job and a rite of passage, but it seemed like the more I managed student behavior, the more the referrals kept coming.

In addition to disciplinary duties, I felt like a private investigator. I conducted more investigations than you could ever imagine into fights, weapons, drugs, and even matters of a sexual nature. On top of all of this, I managed coverage for teachers who were absent frequently. I created rotation schedules, but it often meant dealing with complaints from teachers or even covering classes myself when no one else could or when others refused.

I did all of this while pursuing my doctoral degree in school administration because I wanted to become a principal. I knew I was more than just a disciplinarian or task manager, so I made the decision to turn my challenges into opportunities that allowed me exposure and visibility.

After shifting my mindset, I was seen in a different light by my principal and teachers. The next year, I became a principal.

The mindset shift I embraced was a game-changer. Since then, I've had the opportunity to coach and advise many assistant principals to help them develop the skill set needed to become effective school principals. None of this would have been possible if I had not made the decision to turn my lemons into lemonade.

The purpose of *The Assistant Principal's Path to Promotion: 12 Power Plays to Develop a Winning Mindset, Lead with Impact, and Get Student Results* is to help you develop the skills to become a confident, principal-ready leader, so you can get a promotion and lead your own school.

I've taken the same strategies I've coached and advised countless assistant principals on and put them into this book. You have to be open-minded and prepared to take calculated, strategic risks if you truly want to grow into a principal-ready leader. The advice you'll find here isn't theory; it's been tested in real schools with real results. My goal is for you not just to read these strategies but to implement them, practice them, and build the confidence and skill set you'll need to step into your own principalship.

By the time you finish *The Assistant Principal's Path to Promotion: 12 Power Plays to Develop a Winning Mindset, Lead with Impact, and Get Student Results*, you will be equipped with the tools, strategies, and mindset shifts you need to step confidently into principal-level leadership. You won't just understand what it takes to move from assistant principal to principal, but you'll also have a clear plan and actionable steps that will help you demonstrate your readiness. This book is your guide to moving beyond handling discipline and putting out daily fires to build systems that work and lead with the confidence and vision of a principal, even before you wear the title.

Before you dive in, I want you to see the framework that grounds this entire book.

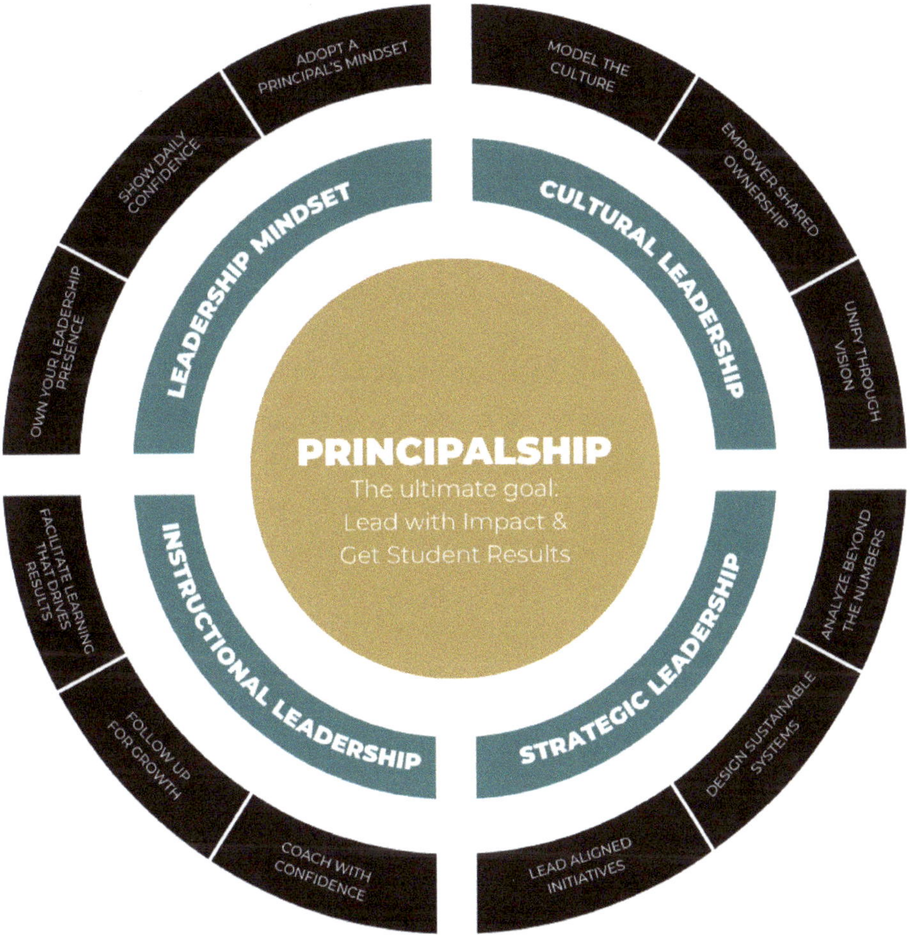

PRINCIPALSHIP
The ultimate goal:
Lead with Impact &
Get Student Results

LEADERSHIP MINDSET

CULTURAL LEADERSHIP

INSTRUCTIONAL LEADERSHIP

STRATEGIC LEADERSHIP

ADOPT A PRINCIPAL'S MINDSET

MODEL THE CULTURE

SHOW DAILY CONFIDENCE

EMPOWER SHARED OWNERSHIP

OWN YOUR LEADERSHIP PRESENCE

UNIFY THROUGH VISION

FACILITATE LEARNING THAT DRIVES RESULTS

ANALYZE BEYOND THE NUMBERS

FOLLOW UP FOR GROWTH

DESIGN SUSTAINABLE SYSTEMS

COACH WITH CONFIDENCE

LEAD ALIGNED INITIATIVES

The Principalship Pathway
Framework™

The Principalship Pathway Framework takes you from where you lead right now to the principalship you're working toward. Every chapter connects to a part of the framework and helps you strengthen your mindset, sharpen your leadership skills, and position yourself for the next level.

At the center of this framework is Principalship, which is the goal you're aiming for but let me be clear. The principalship isn't just about earning a new title. It's about becoming the kind of leader who's ready for that seat because you've done the inner and outer work to grow into it. It's the result of intentional growth, steady reflection, and courageous action right where you are.

Surrounding the principalship are the four key dimensions that drive your growth: Leadership Mindset, Cultural Leadership, Strategic Leadership, and Instructional Leadership. These are the muscles you'll build throughout this book. Each one strengthens a different part of your leadership identity, and together, they form the foundation that will carry you into a principalship with confidence.

- Your Leadership Mindset is where it all starts. It's how you see yourself and how you respond when challenges test your capacity to lead. Without the right mindset, the rest won't hold.
- Cultural Leadership is how you set the tone. It's how you create spaces where people feel seen, supported, and valued.
- Strategic Leadership is how you plan the moves that matter. It's how you see the whole board and align your actions to a bigger vision.
- Instructional Leadership is what builds your credibility. It's how you coach, develop, and grow teachers, so student achievement follows.

The Principalship Pathway Framework reflects the reality of leadership. Your mindset fuels your ability to lead strategically, culturally, and instructionally. Those three pillars, when practiced together, prepare you for what's waiting at the center—a principalship.

As you move through this book, keep this framework in mind. Every story, strategy, and reflection ties back to one or more of these four areas. By the end, you'll not only know what it takes to be principal-ready, but you'll also become the kind of leader who's ready to take that seat with confidence, lead with impact, and get student results!

Your journey to the principalship starts now.
Stay Elevated,

Dr. Bobbie Mills

CHAPTER 1

Wearing the Role
Before It Fits

"Believe in yourself! Have faith in your abilities!"
—Norman Vincent Peale

When I was a younger assistant principal, I was asked to serve as the interim principal of our school over the summer. I was serving in a Title I middle school, one of the largest middle schools in the county. We had over 1,700 students in the building and close to 100 staff members. A new principal had been hired, but they were not able to start until our back-to-school opening staff meeting in August. My zone superintendent had his administrative assistant contact me to schedule a meeting. I had no idea what I was about to walk into. I felt anxious because I thought I was going to be moved to another school, but to my surprise, I was offered the opportunity to serve as my school's interim principal until the new principal arrived.

My zone superintendent said that he had been watching me over the past three years, and he felt that I would be the perfect person to serve in this role temporarily. I graciously accepted, feeling excited.

Here I was with only three years of experience, and I'd been offered an opportunity that I felt would open the door to a principalship for me in the future.

After my meeting was over, I immediately reached out to some veteran principals whom I knew for guidance. They gave me advice and told me they would support me. Most teachers in the building were happy that I had been named to serve as the interim principal and were very supportive. I figured my current skill set was all I needed to open up the school. All I had ever done while I was an assistant principal was discipline and managerial tasks, but I said to myself, *Surely it can't be that hard to open a school for the new school year.* Boy, was I wrong!

There was so much to be done prior to our opening back-to-school meeting. I had to interview and hire teachers, make sure the master schedule was completed, attend principal meetings and professional developments, meet with the other assistant principals and provide them with tasks, and meet with teachers, custodians, cafeteria staff, parents, and community members. My phone was ringing off the hook, and my emails were never-ending. I had gotten to a point where my imposter syndrome kicked in, and I began doubting if I could actually do this. I began to feel as though I was in way over my head and had agreed to take on a role that was two sizes too big for me.

Your mindset is everything. It isn't just a thought you have in the moment; it's the lens through which you interpret every challenge and opportunity. When you step into a leadership role that feels bigger than you, your mindset determines whether you shrink back or rise up. Every decision you make, conversation you have, and action you take is practice for the role you're growing into. Wearing the role before it fits starts first in your mind, and you have to see yourself as capable before others can trust you to lead.

I had to choose between two paths. I could either shift my mindset and put strategies in place, so I could successfully open the school or allow my imposter syndrome to sabotage my chances of ever being noticed again. I took a step back and took many deep breaths. I remembered that I was chosen to lead. If my zone superintendent had confidence in me to lead my school, then why was I doubting myself?

Every time self-doubt tried to rear its ugly head, I remembered that I was chosen, and I wore the role of interim principal before it actually fit. My zone superintendent could have easily had one of his directors come to the school and serve as the interim principal, but he saw something in me that at the time I didn't even see in myself—I was a leader and a damn good one!

After successfully opening the school and preparing our back-to-school opening staff meeting, I realized that being a leader was more than buses, books, and behinds.

I discovered that cultural leadership was paramount to this undertaking for me. I had to learn how to navigate relationships at every level, building trust with teachers and listening to the community's concerns. I realized that culture wasn't just about morale; it was about creating a sense of belonging and shared responsibility, so people felt seen, valued, and willing to follow the vision.

At the same time, I found myself pushed into instructional leadership before I expected it. With the new principal yet to arrive, I had to step up and speak clearly to our staff about where instruction needed to go. This wasn't about repeating empty buzzwords; I had to really grasp how effective teaching looked and offer teachers practical, meaningful ways to improve their practice. To me, instructional leadership meant connecting the day-to-day work teachers do with the results we want to see for our students.

I realized I couldn't lead instruction without first leaning into strategic leadership. I had to step back, sift through the data, and really figure out the true needs of our students, staff, and community. That meant spotting patterns, anticipating roadblocks, and planning carefully, so every decision aligned with a bigger goal. Looking back, I can see the same pattern that I teach today—strategy sets the stage, instruction drives the action, and culture keeps everything together.

What this taught me was that wearing the role before it fits is about embracing leadership even when self-doubt and limited experience make you uncomfortable. Sometimes, growth happens when you simply show up in the role before you fully feel ready. When you believe in yourself enough for others to see it, that voice in your head starts to catch up with the opportunity you've been given.

I knew an assistant principal who was unexpectedly asked by her principal to lead a schoolwide professional development on small group instruction. Teachers were already griping and complaining, saying they had no time to implement the initiative. They felt that the way they were teaching was just fine (although their data said different).

As the assistant principal began her presentation, she was petrified. She did not feel qualified because she was only in her first year, and she was surrounded by veteran teachers. Some of them had over 15 years of experience. She thought, *Who am I to tell them to use small group instruction? They have been teaching longer than I have been in this role, and I know they aren't going to listen to me.*

She stumbled through the opening of the session. Her voice was shaky, and she tried to rely heavily on the pre-prepared slides. The teachers knew she was nervous, and they began whispering to one another, which only fueled her insecurity. Halfway through her presentation, she shifted. Instead of telling the teachers they were going to implement small group instruction during their classes, she asked them to share what was working in their classrooms, and she facilitated the conversation by capturing strategies on chart paper. She then shared data with the teachers and explained how using small group instruction could help them close more gaps in student achievement than using whole group instruction alone. The session ended with teachers walking away with a plan to implement small group instruction, and they exchanged best practices with one another. Several teachers even thanked her afterward for creating a space where their voices were valued.

The assistant principal realized that wearing the role before it fit didn't mean having all the answers. She made a shift and stepped into a space where she leaned on collaboration until her confidence caught up. Her shift from insecurity to facilitation showed her that leadership was about creating opportunities for others to shine and not proving that she knew everything.

Wearing the role before it fits doesn't mean waiting until you feel fully prepared. It means stepping into uncomfortable moments, finding your voice, and leading through collaboration until your confidence grows into the position you've been given.

Visit www.myappath.com/principal-ready-confidence-checklist to access the Principal-Ready Confidence Checklist to help you become principal-ready.

Here are strategies for you to use to wear the role before it fits:

Strategy #1:

Embrace the fear. Self-doubt is a sign you're growing. When you find yourself in roles that feel a little too big, like stepping in as interim principal or leading PD for seasoned teachers, it's natural for imposter syndrome to sneak in. However, that discomfort is not something to fear. It's a signal that you're stretching, learning, and stepping into something new. If others have trusted you with the opportunity, it's because they already see something strong in you before you see it yourself, so when that doubt shows up, don't treat it like a stop sign. Let it remind you that you're heading somewhere important.

Strategy #2:

Lead through collaboration. You don't need to know everything to wear the role. Like the AP who shifted a shaky PD session into a teacher-led conversation, lean into collaboration. Lean into the power of collaboration: ask good questions, spotlight others' strengths, and tie their insights back to the bigger picture or the data. Leadership isn't about being the loudest or the most knowledgeable. It's about creating clarity, building trust, and helping the team move forward together.

Strategy #3:

Keep cultural, strategic, and instructional leadership at the center of everything you do. When you're stepping into a role that doesn't quite fit yet, it's tempting to focus on the to-do list—tasks, schedules, logistics. However, leadership isn't just about keeping things running. It's about holding the line between culture, instruction, and strategy. That means building trust and relationships, staying focused on teaching and learning, and thinking ahead with a clear plan. Before you make a call, pause and ask yourself, *Am I considering all three?*

- How will this impact the culture of the school?
- What strategic outcome will it move us toward?
- How does it connect to instructional growth?

CHAPTER 2

Second in Command, First in Mind

"Doing the best at this moment puts you in the best place for the next moment."
—Oprah Winfrey

A new assistant principal started working at a school where discipline referrals were through the roof. The teachers' first course of action was to write a referral or send the student to the office to see the assistant principal. The principal was consumed with attending district meetings and trying to focus on improving the academic achievement of students, leaving little time to address the issue. Most people assumed the assistant principal's job was just to handle discipline by processing referrals and handing out consequences.

The assistant principal, however, thought differently. She knew that in order for academic achievement to improve, they were going to have to get a handle on the discipline. Instead of just reacting, she started thinking like a principal would. She began asking what the root causes of student behaviors were and what systems she could put into place to address them.

She analyzed the referral data and noticed that the majority came from one grade level during transitions between classes. She pulled the teachers together and shared the data with them. Next, she completed a root cause analysis activity with the teachers, which exposed some truths that they hadn't even realized because for so long, they had lived in a culture with a 'shoot first' mentality instead of finding out the why behind the behaviors they were seeing. After completing this activity, the assistant principal and teachers worked together and developed a hallway supervision schedule and partnered with the school counselor to teach quick conflict-resolution strategies during advisory.

Within a month, referrals dropped by nearly 40%. Teachers were taking the time to actually talk to students and use restorative practices. They began establishing relationships with parents and contacting them to let them know about their students' progress not only for behaviors, but also for academics. Her principal was impressed with her way of thinking and praised her initiative during a staff meeting, saying, "This is what it looks like to lead beyond the task in front of you."

Your mindset as an assistant principal determines whether you're seen as a helper who reacts to problems or a leader who drives solutions. By shifting from just handling referrals to thinking like a principal, you position yourself as more than second in command. You become the thought partner your school needs to move forward. This mindset shift is what gets you noticed, trusted, and remembered for leadership beyond discipline.

Visit www.myappath.com/Second-in-Command-Conversation-Starter-Toolkit to access the Second in Command Conversation Starter Toolkit to help you start powerful conversations with teachers, so you can lead like a principal.

Later, when it came time for the principal pool to open, the assistant principal made the cut. Her principal was able to advocate for her to his superintendent and executive cabinet because she was not remembered for just handling referrals. She was memorable for thinking like a principal and creating a system that helped solve a schoolwide problem.

From this story, I learned that knowing how to use data in the right way is what truly matters. When the assistant principal dug into the data and looked at trends, she was creating a leadership moment. By leading teachers through a root cause analysis, she helped them see things they hadn't noticed and shifted the culture from blaming students to understanding them. That process allowed her to build a system that solved the problem and, at the same time, grow her teachers' capacity. She did all this while being second in command but leading like a principal in her mind.

At one point during my assistant principal career, I was moved to another middle school that was transitioning to become a 6–12 school. Each year, the school grew by a grade level. When our district released end-of-course data, our tenth grade's biology scores were lower than any other school in the district. My principal was new to the school and was focused on trying to get discipline under control.

Seeing that my principal had tunnel vision with this area of focus, I used this opportunity to demonstrate my instructional leadership. I asked if I could lead the PLC for the biology teachers. Now, I had never taught biology a day in my life! I was a former English language arts teacher, and I was a great teacher who always had amazing test scores. When I asked her if I could take the lead, she looked at me hesitantly, but she agreed.

I first met with the biology teachers and shared the data with them. I listened to their concerns and together, we completed a strengths, weaknesses, opportunities for growth, and threats (SWOT) analysis. They shared with me the resources they needed in order to make their lessons more hands-on. During PLC meetings, we collaborated and created weekly common assessments in order to be able to progress monitor students' growth and to determine which standards students needed to be re-engaged with. What I brought to the table during the PLC meetings wasn't content knowledge. I brought strategies I used as an English language arts teacher.

I coached the teachers on how to strategically place students in groups, so they could have discourse with one another about the lesson. During PLCs, I showed the teachers how to properly unpack standards and focus on priority standards that were heavily weighted on the end-of-course exam, so they could get the biggest bang for their buck with their students. I shared with them how to take the data and use it to form small group instruction during their classes. I frequently conducted classroom walkthroughs and provided growth feedback to each of the teachers.

Before I started working with the teachers, their first semester cohort of students' end-of-course exam data overall was 32%. After working with me for a semester, we jumped to 67%, which was a 35% increase. Once the data came out, my principal said to me, "This is really huge, what you did."

I didn't just sit back and wait for my principal to tell me what to do. Sure, I was still second in command, but I was thinking as though I was first in command in my mind, and I led instructionally like a principal. Even though biology wasn't my content area, I realized that strong instructional leadership was transferable.

Eventually, I applied for a principalship, and I was hired to be the principal at an elementary school. During my interview, I used this example when they asked me what I had done to improve instruction at my school. Here's some advice. When you interview for a principalship, superintendents want to know what you have done to improve a school's culture, how you have planned strategically, and how you've led instructionally. They do not want to hear about what your principal did. By working with those biology teachers, I was able to showcase all three and improve student achievement.

Here are three ways you can still be second in command, but you can lead first in your mind:

Strategy #1:

Lead with data and not just discipline. Don't wait for your principal to direct your every move. Use data to identify patterns and lead the work yourself. Whether it's behavior referrals or academic performance, dig into the numbers to uncover root causes. Then, bring teachers into the process through collaborative activities like a root cause analysis or SWOT. This not only creates systems that solve problems, but it also grows teachers' capacity and credibility in your leadership.

Strategy #2:

Don't be afraid to step into content areas outside your comfort zone. You don't need to be a content expert to lead instruction. What teachers often need most are strategies for grouping, unpacking standards, progress monitoring, and using data to adjust instruction. By bringing transferable teaching practices and strong facilitation skills to PLCs, you can guide teachers to higher student achievement results even in subjects you've never taught. Instructional leadership is about growing people, not knowing every detail of the content.

Strategy #3:

Act like an assistant principal, but think like a principal. Being second in command doesn't mean staying in the background. When your principal's focus is elsewhere, step up and lead in ways that complement their vision. Use those moments to demonstrate that you can manage culture, plan strategically, and drive instruction. These are the very examples you'll need in interviews for principalships, and they will set you apart as someone who already thinks and acts like the leader of the school.

CHAPTER 3

Be a Strong Number Two

"It is literally true that you can succeed best and quickest
by helping others to succeed."
—Napoleon Hill

I know an assistant principal who stepped in alongside a brand-new principal. With seven years under her belt, she quickly saw just how overwhelming those first months can be. The principal was being pulled in every direction. He was handling teacher evaluations, parent concerns, discipline issues, district meetings, and the endless day-to-day operations that kept his school running. He was working hard to build a vision, but the daily grind was taking a toll on him.

That's when the AP decided to step up. One afternoon, after watching the principal spend hours trying to manage classroom visits, she said, "Let me take this off your plate." Within a week, she put together a walkthrough schedule that ensured every classroom got regular visits without the principal having to micromanage. Teachers no longer wondered if or when leadership might drop by, and the principal could finally trust that instructional walkthroughs were happening every day.

She didn't stop there. The AP kicked off a weekly instructional focus, sending out clear updates every Friday: "Next week, we're focusing on student engagement strategies. Here's what to highlight, and here's what the admin will be looking for during walkthroughs." That simple step aligned the staff and gave real momentum to the principal's vision in the classrooms.

To lighten the load even more, she started drafting the weekly parent newsletter. The principal gave the final okay, but she handled the messaging—sharing updates, celebrating wins, keeping parents connected. One day, after reading through the newsletter, the principal looked up and said, "You're a life saver." Those words said it all. For the principal, it was not just about getting tasks done; it was about the freedom she gave him to focus on leading.

She went even deeper and scheduled one-on-one chats with teachers. She did not do this to evaluate, but to listen. Teachers opened up about what was working, what wasn't, and where they needed support. Using diagnostic data from earlier in the year, she helped teachers connect the dots: "Here's where our students are now. Let's talk about what that means for your instruction." Those conversations brought clarity to teachers and gave the principal a stronger base to build on.

What stands out is that these weren't just routine tasks. They were leadership moves. By setting up structures for walkthroughs, focusing instructional priorities, communicating with parents, coaching teachers, and using data to guide decisions, the AP was building her own leadership muscles in instruction, culture, and strategy, all while backing up her principal.

She never tried to overshadow him. Instead, she amplified his leadership. By taking on the structures, communication, and data-driven work, she freed the principal to focus on the school's vision, relationships, and the big picture. She became the kind of number two every principal dreams of—not just following orders but pushing the work forward.

Being a strong number two is about more than carrying out tasks. It's about intentionally carving out your leadership lane while supporting your principal's vision. The mindset you bring determines whether you're seen as just helping out or as someone capable of leading side by side with the principal. Every structure you build, every communication you streamline, and every coaching conversation you have is not just support; it's leadership in motion. Those daily moves are what position you as principal-ready.

What I learned from watching this is that being a strong number two isn't about competing with your principal or trying to outshine them. It's about lifting up their leadership in ways that make the whole school stronger. When you do that, you earn trust and respect, and you grow your own influence with teachers, students, and parents. That's the real power of being a strong number two. When you raise your leader, you raise yourself, too.

Visit www.myappath.com/The-Strong-Number-Two-Leadership-Moves-Checklist to access The Strong Number Two Leadership Moves Checklist to help you amplify your principal's vision while strengthening your own leadership.

One day, my principal suddenly got called out because a zone superintendent had stopped by unexpectedly. My principal asked me to continue the meeting. I felt a little nervous because we were discussing a new instructional framework initiative that the staff was not sold on. When I got up, a veteran teacher made a negative comment, expressing her feelings about the initiative. This was something she would not have said had the principal been in the room. I realized that the teachers felt a little too comfortable around me if they were comfortable enough to make that statement. After the teacher made the negative comment, others laughed and chimed in, but I knew I had to steer the conversation back to the original focus.

I stood tall and put the focus back on best practices. I explained why this initiative was important and backed it up with data.

Some teachers weren't comfortable with their data, and they still brought a negative attitude to the table, but I kept steering the conversation back to what really mattered—the students. For me, grounding every discussion in students' needs ensured that personal frustrations, pushback on accountability, or negativity didn't throw us off course. Data can feel uncomfortable, but it's never about proving anyone wrong. It's about figuring out what our students need to grow. By bringing the focus back to student outcomes, I reminded everyone that our decisions, strategies, and energy have to serve one goal—helping students succeed. When adults shift their attention away from themselves and onto the kids, it breaks down defensiveness and creates a shared space to move forward together.

After the meeting was over, other teachers came to me and told me that I did a great job standing my ground by using the data and talking about the best interest of the students instead of going down a rabbit hole and talking about why others didn't want to do it based on their personal emotions.

The lesson I learned from that experience is that being a strong number two means you're trusted to carry your principal's vision even when they're not in the room. People respond to how you show up when it's time to lead. When the principal steps out, everyone's watching to see if you can keep the same standards, stay focused on the students, and confidently steer the conversation forward. That moment isn't just about you. It's a reflection of the school's vision as a whole. A strong second in command doesn't just fill a gap; they bring stability, model how alignment looks, and show that the work keeps moving no matter who's in the room. Doing this builds trust with both the staff and the principal, proving that you're dependable in the moment and ready to take on bigger leadership roles.

Remember, even though you are second in command, it is important to exhibit strong leadership qualities, so you can step up when the time comes and continue to focus on your school's vision and mission.

Here are three strategies to help you be a strong number two:

Strategy #1:

Lead with courage. Stand behind your principal's vision openly, but don't shy away from calling out negativity or pushback when it comes up. When tough conversations happen, keep the focus on what's best for the students and the school's mission. Showing courage in those moments tells staff you're not just there to fill a role; you're there to protect the work and lead with real impact.

Strategy #2:

Carry that vision every day, no matter who's in the room. Don't wait for the principal to be there to model what the school stands for. Step into meetings, conversations, and decision-making moments with the same clarity and expectations they would bring. When staff see steady leadership, they start to believe the school's direction isn't tied to one person; it's a shared commitment everyone owns.

Strategy #3:

Get ahead of the game. Don't wait for someone to tell you what to do. Stay at least 10 steps ahead. A strong second in command doesn't just put out fires; they anticipate challenges and set up systems before problems even show up. Leading with that mindset proves to the principal and staff that you can keep things steady and lead effectively.

Voices From the
Path Mindset Interview

Name: Donovan Kent

Title: Assistant Principal

School District: Winston-Salem Forsyth County Schools

1. What was the biggest mindset shift you had to make when you first became an assistant principal?

The biggest shift was moving from being responsible for my own classroom to being responsible for the larger school community. As a teacher, I measured success by the growth, proficiency, and relationships that I fostered with my own students. As an AP, I had to broaden my lens and recognize that every decision—whether about academics, safety, school culture, or building relationships—affects hundreds of stakeholders (students, teachers, and families). That meant learning to delegate, prioritize, and lead through others, rather than trying to do everything myself.

2. How did that mindset change affect the way you led your school Community?

It made me more intentional about how I use my time and how I empower others. Instead of being reactive, I began to schedule my priorities—classroom visits, instructional coaching, and building relationships with staff and students. By delegating effectively and trusting my team, I could focus more on instructional leadership and long-term goals, rather than just putting out fires. This shift helped me model balance and clarity for my staff, while ensuring the most important needs of our school community were consistently addressed.

3. Can you share a challenge where your mindset made the difference between reacting as an AP versus thinking like a principal?

One challenge was handling a serious student conflict that had the potential to escalate into a larger safety issue. My initial instinct as an AP was to manage it quickly and move on, but I stopped and asked myself, "How would a good principal approach this?" Instead of just reacting, I worked with the SRO, counselors, and behavior specialist to address the root causes, involve families, and put supports in place. That broader, principal-level mindset turned a potential crisis into an opportunity to strengthen systems and relationships.

4. **What advice would you give other APs who want to grow their leadership mindset now before becoming principals?**

My advice would be to think bigger than your current role. Don't just solve problems, look at how systems and structures can prevent them. Prioritize what matters most. Safety, instructional leadership, and positive relationships must always be at the top of the list. Practice delegation. Leadership is not about doing everything yourself; it's about building capacity in others. Be reflective. Learn from mistakes. Stay flexible and don't take setbacks personally. Every challenge prepares you to make a greater impact.

5. **You've worked with Dr. Mills. How did her guidance help you strengthen your leadership mindset, and would you recommend that other assistant principals work with her?**

Absolutely. Dr. Mills helped me shift from simply working harder to working smarter. Through her mentoring, I learned how to prioritize effectively, organize my day with balance, and make intentional time for instructional leadership. She encouraged me to delegate more, trust my team, and build systems that sustain themselves. Her guidance also pushed me to think beyond the AP role and practice leading like a principal. I would strongly recommend her to any AP who wants to accelerate their growth and strengthen their leadership mindset.

CHAPTER 4

Leading the Culture
You Want to See

"What you do has far
greater impact than what you say."
—Stephen Covey

A principal I know had a food fight in her school cafeteria one day. She walked into the cafeteria and saw food and milk being thrown across the cafeteria while students were running around and screaming. Teachers were trying to stop them to no avail. It was pure chaos. When the students saw the principal walk into the cafeteria, they stopped in their tracks and waited for her reaction. Instead of screaming at the top of her lungs, she remained calm, got a broom from the closet, and started sweeping the floor. She did not utter one word. The cafeteria was dead silent. Even the teachers were confused. The students couldn't believe that she was not flipping out. Then, suddenly, a chain reaction occurred. One by one, the students slowly started to help the principal clean the cafeteria.

After school was over, the principal called an emergency grade level meeting with the teachers to debrief what had happened. After listening to the teachers complain about how the students didn't listen to them and how they were so disrespectful, she explained that there was a culture and climate problem within the grade level, and the actions that took place in the cafeteria were speaking loud and clear. The principal explained the difference between culture and climate—culture was the behavior, language, and expectations they carried on the hallway, and climate was the mood. She told the teachers that the climate was dictating how the students were acting because the mood did not include having high expectations. The principal worked alongside the teachers to strategize how to reset expectations. They established how to enter and leave classrooms, how to line up in the hallways, what the students' voice levels should be in certain areas in the school, and how to communicate with parents. Then, she gathered the students in a grade level assembly and spoke about having pride in their school, and she shared how their behavior did not reflect the culture she expected them to uphold. She told the students that eating in the cafeteria was a privilege that they would have to earn back by demonstrating they could follow simple rules and procedures.

For a time, the students were required to eat in their classrooms. Gradually, as they demonstrated respect, order, and responsibility, they earned the privilege of returning to the cafeteria. Over time, their behavior aligned with the culture the principal wanted to see, not because she demanded it through fear, but because she showed them what leadership looked like in action, and she set a clear standard for what was expected moving forward.

Leading culture isn't about being controlling. It's about modeling the behaviors, routines, and values you expect others to live out. When you position yourself as the model, the mirror, and the motivator, you create a ripple effect that empowers staff and students to rise to a higher standard. That's how you begin shifting from managing culture to truly leading it.

What I took away from this is that real leadership in shaping school culture comes from showing the behavior and mindset you want to see in others. As a leader, you set the tone in your building with everything you say and do. People are always watching, not just when you're giving directions, but they are especially watching when you're handling the tough, stressful moments. Leadership isn't about words. It's about what you *show*.

Visit www.myappath.com/The-Culture-Leadership-Playbook to access the Culture Leadership Playbook to help you build, model, and sustain the culture you want to create.

When the principal calmly grabbed a broom during a chaotic moment, that action spoke louder than any speech ever could. It said loud and clear: *Dignity, responsibility, and keeping your cool are non-negotiable here.* That one simple act didn't just stop a food fight; it changed the way students and staff thought about leadership and accountability. Culture isn't shaped by what you demand. It is shaped by what you model. People will follow your lead.

When I was an assistant principal, my principal established morning meetings for teachers. This was a time for teachers to come together before the classes began each day and get communication from the principal and APs on events that were taking place that day or week. Everyone got together for 15 to 20 minutes before students arrived. This was put into place because teachers were complaining about a lack of communication and low staff morale, and they said they didn't know what was happening in the building.

My principal didn't want culture to be something only the admin team carried. He believed it had to be everyone's responsibility because culture can't last if it's resting on the shoulders of principals and assistant principals. When teachers, staff, and leaders at every level get involved, the message becomes clear: This is our school, and we all shape its climate. When people own it, they buy in, and it is the buy-in that brings people together.

Each week, different grade levels took turns leading daily motivation activities followed by announcements from the principal, assistant principal, or department heads. This made the staff feel more connected, and it kept everyone in the loop about what was going on around the building. That consistent participation built trust and helped everyone see themselves as contributors to the culture and not just people affected by it.

Morale improved, and staff started feeling more in tune not only with what was happening in the building but also with what their colleagues were doing in their classrooms. This transparency created a stronger community feeling. Teachers stopped feeling isolated, and they started to see themselves as part of a bigger team. Meetings became a place where collaboration felt normal and where teachers could share successful strategies from other grade levels, understand how their work linked to the bigger school goals, and feel recognized for their efforts. It was also a great time to celebrate wins, big or small. Recognizing birthdays, teaching successes, and student achievements sends out positive vibes that culture isn't just about fixing problems; it's about celebrating progress, whether personal or professional. Over time, these shared moments built pride, belonging, and a sense of collective ownership of the school's success.

This is where you have a unique opportunity. You don't just keep culture running. You have the chance to hardwire it into the fabric of the school. When you create routines, invite shared ownership, and consistently model what matters, you shift the story from what leadership expects to this is who we are as a school. That mindset not only strengthens today's culture but also positions you as a leader who knows how to build sustainable systems, which is one of the key marks of being principal-ready.

This experience taught me that leading the culture you want means building rhythms and routines that keep everyone informed, motivated, and engaged. Culture thrives when you have regular, predictable practices such as staff meetings, recognition rituals, and clear communication that ground the community. Those routines send the message that everyone belongs, and consistency is more important than occasional big events.

Culture can't just be a leadership checkbox. It has to be a shared responsibility. When teachers, staff, and leaders all see themselves as caretakers of culture, it stops being just words in a handbook or a statement on a wall. It comes alive every day through actions and interactions. That shared ownership keeps culture strong, even when leaders change, or tough times hit.

Remember, the culture you build today shapes the whole school community tomorrow. Every choice, every routine, and every action you model either builds trust and connection or chips away at it. That's why leading culture takes intention, presence, and teamwork. Culture isn't what you say; it's what you do. The sum of those choices creates a place where students and staff can thrive.

Here are three strategies you can use:

Strategy #1:

Model what you want to see. Culture is caught, not taught. If you expect punctuality, positivity, and professionalism, you have to show it yourself every day. From greeting students in the morning to modeling how to react under pressure, you set the tone. When you live the culture you want, others start to follow.

Strategy #2:

Spread ownership. Don't let culture be just an admin job. Invite teachers, staff, and even students to take the lead on recognition programs, motivational moments, or community-building events. When everyone feels responsible for the culture, it sticks, and it lasts, even when you're not there.

Strategy #3:

Build culture into daily routines. Culture is in the little things, like how you show up, how you talk, and how you treat people. Be on time, engage positively with students and staff, and use every opportunity (staff meetings, PLCs, announcements, celebrations) to reinforce your school's values and vision. Set up systems like shared celebrations and open communication that make culture visible and real. Over time, those routines become the heartbeat of your school, shaping how everyone feels and acts.

The Culture Can't Rely On You

"True leadership is when you create an environment
where people don't need you to be
there to do their best work."
—Simon Sinek

When I was an assistant principal, I had to attend assistant principal meetings off campus once a month. They only lasted the first half of the morning; however, the whole time I was at the meetings, I kept my laptop open to check emails, and I had my phone on vibrate because something always happened when I left. Whenever I returned, it always seemed like all hell broke loose. I returned to having to deal with fights, referrals pouring out of my mailbox, teachers coming to me crying and upset, asking me where I had been, and saying I could never leave the school again. I couldn't understand why whenever I was off campus, everything fell apart. After careful reflection, I came to the conclusion that I was the only person who held the power.

The truth hit me hard. My grade level's school culture was revolving around me. Without even realizing it, I'd become the go-to problem solver. I was the one holding the keys to discipline, decisions, and direction. Teachers leaned on me because I'd set up systems that depended on me instead of empowering them to step up. The staff didn't have the confidence or ownership to manage things when I wasn't around because I hadn't figured out how to share authority or spread leadership. If the culture can't survive without you, that's not a sign of strength. It's a red flag for dependency. Real power isn't about being the only one who holds it all together. Real power is creating a culture that keeps going strong even when you step away.

I realized I had to build a system on my hallway. Without one, the culture was fragile and too tied to me being physically present to keep things running smoothly. If everything fell apart whenever I left, then I wasn't leading. I was controlling instead. Systems bring stability, predictability, and shared ownership. They let the culture thrive, even if the leader isn't there. By setting clear expectations and giving others roles, I could build capacity in my team, so the school climate didn't ride on me alone.

I met with key teachers and staff members on my hallway and gave them leadership roles such as making sure the halls were clean or ensuring that their colleagues were at their doors during transitions. When I had days off campus, I gave teachers plenty of heads-up, so they could be ready to lead while I was gone. I also checked in with another assistant principal to watch over my hallway. Once I got my teachers involved, problems during my absence dropped dramatically.

Visit www.myappath.com/The-Culture-Independence-Toolkit to access the Culture Independence Toolkit to help you design systems that keep your school's culture independent when you're not in the building.

A school's culture can't be dependent on just one person. It has to be built to run independently. Here is the reality. Principals and assistant principals move all the time. They get promoted or transferred, or they make career changes. If your culture is dependent on you to be the glue that holds everything together, then it will not be sustainable, which is why you need to empower teachers, staff, and even students to take ownership of establishing a positive culture in order to build their leadership capacity. When you focus on building systems and empowering others, you create a culture that thrives whether you're present or not. That shift in thinking positions you as principal-ready because principals don't just solve problems. They create structures where the work continues and grows, even in their absence. Leadership means creating systems that keep your influence strong even when you're not in the building.

I've seen this play out elsewhere too. At one school, an assistant principal took pride in running a reading PLC. She set the agendas, led discussions, and analyzed data for teachers. At first, it seemed smooth and efficient. Teachers liked the clear direction and organization, but when she had to cover lunch duty for a few weeks, the PLCs lost their rhythm. Meetings stalled. Data talks dried up, and teachers said they didn't know what to do without her.

When she came back, she realized her leadership had created dependence, not true collaboration. By doing all the work, she'd unintentionally stopped teachers from developing the skills to lead data talks, set goals, and hold one another accountable. The culture wasn't collaborative; it was fragile. If it collapses when the leader steps away, it was never strong in the first place.

She learned that doing all the heavy lifting might feel effective short-term, but it weakens culture long-term. Running every PLC herself seemed like she was saving time and modeling best practices, but really, it told teachers the work couldn't move forward without her. That was a humbling wake-up call. A strong instructional culture isn't one where the AP is the hub of knowledge and direction; it's where teachers own the process.

She realized her job wasn't to be the hero in every meeting, Her role was building leadership in others. Teachers needed to know how to analyze data, set meaningful goals, and hold each other accountable. If her stepping away meant collaboration stopped, then what they had wasn't really culture; it was a crutch. True instructional culture has to be strong enough to thrive without you.

When you intentionally step back and give teachers the tools, confidence, and space to lead, you stop being the bottleneck and start being the architect of sustainable culture. That mindset of designing independence rather than dependence is what transforms you from a manager into a leader who is ready to take on a principalship.

Here are three strategies that really help:

Strategy #1:

Share the ownership by spreading leadership. Don't try to be the center of every decision or process. Give teachers, staff, and students clear leadership roles. Make teachers PLC facilitators, hallway leaders, or grade reps. When leadership is shared, culture doesn't fall apart if you're not there because others are ready and trusted to step up.

Strategy #2:

Build systems, not habits. If something only works because you're running it, it's not a real system. It's a habit tied to you. Write down daily procedures such as arrival, transitions, dismissal, discipline flow, and communication and make sure several people know how to handle them. Systems need to be predictable and repeatable, not person-dependent. That way, culture stays strong, no matter who's around.

Strategy #3:

Grow teachers' problem-solving skills. Don't jump in to fix every problem yourself. Instead, coach teachers on handling discipline, having effective parent conversations, or conducting data analysis. Push them to bring solutions, not just problems. Giving teachers the tools and confidence to act builds a resilient culture where leadership isn't just in your office; it's everywhere.

CHAPTER 6

Two Cultures, One School

"A house divided against itself cannot stand."
—Abraham Lincoln

When I was an assistant principal, I worked at a unique school that started with grades six through eight and added a grade each year until it became a full high school. What began as an exciting opportunity quickly turned into a challenge no one really saw coming. As the school evolved, the ninth through twelfth graders got labeled "the academy," while six through eight stuck with "the traditional middle school." At first, it was just a name, but over time, those labels created two very different worlds inside the same building.

The high school side quickly became the star of the show. Classrooms were freshly painted with bright, modern colors. They brought in sleek furniture that supported flexible learning, and students got brand-new Chromebooks to use in class. The message was clear. This was the future—the part everyone was most excited about.

Meanwhile, the middle school side told a very different story. The walls were faded. They were in serious need of a fresh coat of paint. Kids sat in old, traditional desks that felt outdated compared to the high school's new spaces. Even though Chromebooks were promised, middle schoolers had to wait until the following year for theirs. Teachers and students noticed the difference, and it didn't take long before the middle school kids started feeling like second-class citizens in their own school.

The problem wasn't just resources. It was starting to affect the culture. Middle school teachers were frustrated, feeling overlooked and under-valued. Kids picked up on that vibe and started comparing themselves to the high school students down the hall. Instead of one school community, two very different cultures were taking shape under the same roof—one feeling prioritized and privileged, the other feeling forgotten and left behind.

Visit www.myappath.com/Culture-Diagnostic to access the Culture Diagnostic to help you identify warning signs of cultural divides and take action before they grow.

As the gap between the academy and the middle school became more obvious, I knew I couldn't just ignore the growing frustration. Teachers were quietly complaining that their students were getting the short end of the stick, and middle schoolers were openly asking why they didn't get the same perks as the high schoolers. The divide was only getting bigger, and if we didn't tackle it, it was going to poison the whole school's culture.

The first thing I did was sit down with my principal and lay it all out— what I was hearing from teachers and what I was seeing in the building. Morale was slipping among middle school teachers. Students were comparing themselves, and tension between the two wings was reaching a breaking point. I told my principal, "If we don't address this now, it's going to turn into resentment. We can't build one school with two cultures fighting for attention." Together, we worked on better ways to communicate the long-term plan, so staff would feel assured the middle school wasn't being forgotten.

I also started having real, honest conversations with the middle school teachers. I made sure they knew I heard their frustrations, but I also tried to shift the story. "Yeah, the high school wing has new paint and furniture, but our students deserve that too, and our job is to get them ready, so they can take advantage of those resources when they move up. The work you're doing is preparing them for what's ahead."

I reminded them that resources were on the way, and their voices mattered in shaping how the middle school rollout would happen. To fight that "left out" feeling, I teamed up with some teachers to create quick wins. We rearranged classrooms to make better use of space, added small touches like bulletin boards and displays to brighten up the hallways, and started highlighting middle school achievements more during staff meetings and announcements. It wasn't the same as Chromebooks or new furniture, but those little changes gave teachers and students a sense of pride and ownership over their part of the building.

What this taught me is that resource gaps don't just impact teaching. They shape the whole culture. When one group feels prioritized, and another feels forgotten, the school naturally splits into "haves" and "have nots." As an assistant principal, I realized my job wasn't just pointing out the problem but leading the effort to close the gap. That meant standing up for fairness with my principal, giving frustrated teachers a voice, and creating small wins, so everyone felt valued while we worked toward bigger changes. Culture can't grow when people feel invisible, or they feel like second-class citizens. True leadership means making sure every teacher and student feels like they belong to the same school community. You can't have two cultures under one roof. You should only have one shared vision that builds a foundation for real success.

At another school, a very different challenge unfolded when a new principal was brought in to turn around a low-performing school, which made the district hopeful. This principal had a solid reputation for pushing academic growth and getting results, even in tough situations. However, soon after he arrived, changes started happening that no one really expected. A lot of the veteran teachers began to leave. Some weren't sure about the new direction. Others were worried about the added pressure from new leadership, and a few just didn't believe the school could really turn around.

When the new school year kicked off, the principal brought along a team of teachers from his old school. They were confident and loyal to him, and they bought into his vision. That confidence, however, quickly morphed into something else—a sense that they were the ones who were going to "save" the school. In their eyes, the teachers who stayed behind were part of the problem. The message, whether spoken or not, was clear: "You couldn't fix it so now we're here to do the job."

That attitude created a split right away. The existing staff felt dismissed and undervalued. They'd been holding down the fort in a tough school for years, often without much recognition or support, and now, they were being painted as ineffective. Meanwhile, the new teachers stuck together, proud of their "turnaround team" status, but they were completely unaware of the resentment brewing around them.

Instead of moving forward as one school, two cultures quickly formed—the new teachers who felt superior because of their past success and the veteran teachers who felt like strangers in their own building. Collaboration broke down. Trust plummeted, and students could sense the tension. The very culture the principal was brought in to fix was now fractured.

The assistant principal, one of the original staff members, noticed what was happening right away. In meetings, she saw veteran teachers on one side, quiet and guarded, while new teachers dominated discussions, sometimes dismissing the school's past approaches. In the halls, she overheard things like, "We've always done it this way," clashing with, "That's why this school is failing." The divide was threatening any progress.

One afternoon, after a tense leadership meeting, she pulled the principal aside and said, "We have two cultures here—the staff who stayed feels shut out and the new staff thinks they're here to rescue everyone. We can't build a unified vision if people are fighting over whose culture is right. If we don't fix this, we won't get anywhere." The principal, focused on results, admitted he saw the split, but he hadn't realized how badly it was hurting morale. He gave her the go-ahead to lead the charge in fixing it.

The assistant principal started by creating spaces where both groups had to work together. She reorganized PLCs, so veteran and new teachers teamed up to analyze student work and plan lessons. She made sure responsibilities were shared, giving both sides a chance to show what they knew and to learn from each other. When new teachers brought ideas from the principal's old school, she reminded them to listen as much as they spoke, highlighting that veteran teachers had valuable knowledge about their students and community.

Behind the scenes, she built relationships by meeting with teachers one-on-one from both groups, affirming their strengths and challenging their biases. At staff meetings, she celebrated wins from both the new and veteran teachers, sending a clear message that everyone mattered in the school's turnaround.

Slowly, the story started to change. The "rescue squad" began to respect the commitment of the veteran teachers. The veterans saw that the newcomers weren't trying to erase their work, but they wanted to support them. Gradually, the two groups shifted from two competing cultures to one school moving forward together.

The assistant principal's courage to call out the divide, bring the principal into the conversation, and take steps to bridge the gap was what let the school start healing. She didn't just manage the tension; she led the effort to create one culture, one school.

Culture divides don't fix themselves. They demand leaders willing to call them out, bring people together, and protect unity. If she had ignored the split, resentment would have deepened. Teamwork would have stalled, and students would have suffered. She realized it wasn't enough to just run operations or discipline. Protecting culture is critical, so a school can move forward as one. Real progress doesn't come when one group dominates the other; it happens when both groups unite under the same vision. When that started to happen, momentum returned. Cultural leadership like this is one of the most powerful things an assistant principal can bring. When you can hold competing groups steady under one vision, you're already practicing the leadership that superintendents and school boards look for in a principal.

Here are three strategies you can use:

Strategy #1:

Name the divide and start the conversation. Don't ignore tension between groups. Call it out and bring it into the open. Talk to your principal about what you're seeing. Have honest conversations with teachers about how it's affecting the school. When people feel heard, walls come down, and "us vs. them" shifts to "we're in this together."

Strategy #2:

Create collaboration opportunities. Whether it's between veteran and new teachers or across grade levels, set up structures that force teamwork. Pair teachers in PLCs. Assign cross-grade projects and make sure everyone's voice is heard. Shared work builds respect, and respect builds unity.

Strategy #3:

Push for fairness and celebrate wins, big or small. Division often grows from real or perceived unfairness. As an assistant principal, be the voice that pushes for equitable resources and recognition. In the meantime, create small wins that highlight strengths on both sides. Celebrate achievements publicly to remind everyone they belong to the same school community, no matter where they came from.

Voices From the
Path Cultural Interview

Name: Dr. Sonia Matthew, 2025 Maryland's National Outstanding Assistant Principal of the Year

Title: Assistant Principal

School District: Charles County Public Schools

1. **From your perspective, what role does an assistant principal play in shaping school culture?**

An assistant principal's influence is rooted in relationships and consistency. By actively listening and being accessible, supportive, and fair in every interaction, an AP can cultivate a culture of trust and respect. This means consistently applying school rules, whether in disciplinary matters or in acknowledging successes, to ensure everyone feels they are treated fairly.

For example, when addressing student behavior, a consistent and supportive approach, rather than a purely punitive one, reinforces a culture where students feel seen and heard. Similarly, providing genuine support to teachers who are struggling, rather than just pointing out deficiencies, builds a collaborative and caring staff culture. These consistent, fair interactions, over time, have a powerful, macro effect on the entire school's atmosphere. The core values of respect, fairness, and consistency become the foundation of the school's identity.

2. **Can you share a specific example of when you influenced culture in a positive way at your school?**

I am really proud of a recent initiative I led this year to shift our school culture to be more inclusive. I saw a powerful opportunity to do this by transforming our student news program.

Previously, the program was limited to a small, exclusive group of students. I changed this by opening the opportunity to anyone who was interested in participating and filled out a simple form. This created a more equitable and accessible program. To support the influx of new students, we implemented a leadership training program in which a team of fifth-grade students mentored and guided younger peers. This not only built the leadership capacity of the older students, but it also fostered a "growth mindset" among all participants.

We also introduced new, engaging segments like "Motivational Monday" and "Wellness Wednesday," which recognized positive character traits and emotional well-being instead of just academic achievements. This simple shift created a more inclusive and appreciative environment, allowing a wider range of students to feel valued for their character and effort.

3. How do you balance supporting your principal's vision while also putting your own stamp on culture?

Balancing your principal's vision with your own approach to culture is all about collaboration. You're both playing the same song, but you're each adding your unique flair. The key is to understand the principal's overarching goals and then use your own strengths and personality to implement them in a way that resonates with the school community. For example, if the principal's vision is to improve student attendance, you might put your own stamp on it by creating a fun, incentive-based program that rewards students and classes for their consistency, rather than just issuing punishments for absences. By operating within the principal's framework, you build a united front while also showing genuine leadership and making the work your own.

Advice for Being Seen as a Cultural Leader

To be recognized as a cultural leader and not just a disciplinarian, an AP must be proactive and visible in positive ways. Disciplinary actions are a necessary part of the job, but they shouldn't be the only way people interact with you.

Here are a few pieces of advice:

1. Be present and visible in non-disciplinary settings. Greet students in the hallway. Attend school events and visit classrooms just to observe and offer praise. This helps build positive rapport and shows you're invested in more than just problem-solving.

2. Acknowledge and praise publicly. Write notes of thanks to staff. Call out positive student behavior and make sure people feel seen and appreciated. This demonstrates that you are a source of support and encouragement, not just authority.

3. Lead with empathy and listening. When problems arise, listen first. Take the time to understand the root cause of an issue before jumping to a solution. This shows people you respect their perspective and are a fair-minded leader.

Why Work with Dr. Mills on Building Culture?

For me, it came down to a simple reality: I was a problem-solver, not a leader. I was smart, dedicated, and worked tirelessly, but I felt like I was constantly putting out fires—a teacher would call out sick, a parent would be upset about a grade, or a student would get into a fight. My to-do list was endless, and my vision of being an instructional leader felt like a distant dream. I knew I was managing, but I wasn't leading, and I didn't know how to change that.

I felt the pressure to build a positive school culture, but between managing lunch duty and discipline, when was there time? I heard talk about being data-driven, but my data was fragmented. The gap between what I wanted to be and what my job demanded was wide. This is where Dr. Mills came in.

She didn't just offer advice; she provided a lifeline. She met me where I was, acknowledging how I was feeling, and helped me build a bridge from reactive management to proactive leadership.

Instead of just telling me what to do, Dr. Mills helped me see how my daily actions, like a brief classroom walkthrough or a difficult conversation with a staff member were opportunities to drive instructional growth. She helped me organize my thoughts and my data, turning chaos into clarity. The endless to-do list didn't disappear, but I learned to approach it with a new mindset.

With Dr. Mills' guidance, I didn't just check off boxes; I was equipped with a strategy to build relationships that foster real change. I started seeing my work as less about putting out fires and more about igniting a passion for learning in my school. Dr. Mills provided the tools, the encouragement, and the unwavering belief that I had the potential to be a powerful and compassionate instructional leader.

CHAPTER 7

Have a Seat

"If they don't give you a seat at the table,
bring a folding chair."
—Shirley Chisholm

During a district school improvement meeting, principals and district leaders gathered to review plans for raising math scores and discuss instructional strategies for improving math proficiency. Assistant principals were invited, but most of them sat quietly in the back of the room, taking notes. There was one assistant principal, however, who brought his folding chair and waited for his opportunity to take a seat at the table to discuss instruction. He was known for leading his school's PLC work and getting results.

As the meeting unfolded, several principals shared general ideas that were nothing new: tutoring, extended learning, and reteaching. No one talked about moving the needle by using best teaching practices. The assistant principal whispered to his principal, asking if he could share what he had done with the teachers at their school. The principal nodded and told him to speak up.

Once he got the attention of the room, all eyes were on him. He explained how he had led his math PLCs in breaking down benchmark data by standard, and then he coached teachers to implement targeted small-group instruction around two high-leverage skills. He even shared before-and-after student work samples to illustrate the gains. His approach was replicable and grounded in results. In one quarter under his leadership, his school's math scores had increased by 12 points.

When he shared his school's gains, there was a shift in the room. Other principals turned around and started asking the assistant principal for his process and examples of his PLC agendas. Because he had such significant gains in just one quarter, the district's facilitator later reached out to request that he lead a professional development at their next district-wide PLC training.

As the superintendent closed the meeting, he said, "That's the type of instructional leadership we need across our schools." When the assistant principal sat down, his principal told him, "You now have their attention!"

The assistant principal left that meeting no longer seen just as second in command. Now, he was viewed as an instructional leader who took his seat at the table and belonged there.

From this experience I learned that being invited into the room is one thing, but being trusted to contribute is what earns you credibility. As an assistant principal, every meeting is a stage where you either reinforce the stereotype of being just the disciplinarian or you rewrite it by adding real value to the conversation. You have to add value once you're there and let people see that you have an instructional mindset as an assistant principal, and you're not just in your building to serve as a disciplinarian. The assistant principal didn't wait for someone to call on him or hope his principal would spotlight his work. He found the right moment, spoke up with confidence, and shared a results-driven strategy that showed he belonged at the table. He showed his superintendent, executive leaders, principals, and fellow colleagues that he was credible because he had led PLCs, tracked data, and coached teachers. He backed up his ideas with evidence and shared how it impacted his school's culture.

Visit www.myappath.com/Meeting-Moves-Prep-Guide to access the Meeting Moves Prep Guide to help you walk into meetings ready to contribute with confidence and credibility.

During a district walkthrough at an elementary school, the superintendent arrived with his central office team to observe instruction. The visit was meant to spotlight how schools were implementing the district's improvement plans. The principal and assistant principal came and welcomed the superintendent and his team in the front office, and then they walked down the hallway to do walkthroughs. Most of the leadership team expected the principal to do the talking, but when they entered a math classroom, the superintendent turned to the principal and asked, "What are you doing to support teachers to improve student discourse?"

Before the principal could answer, the assistant principal stepped forward and confidently explained how he had been leading the math PLCs in planning student-centered lessons. Then, he described the specific coaching cycles he had implemented: walkthroughs, feedback, and follow-up. He pointed out evidence of these practices on the walkthrough dashboard they kept in house at their school.

The superintendent was intrigued. Here was this assistant principal taking the lead and having an instructional conversation with him and his team. The superintendent continued to ask follow-up questions, and the assistant principal responded with concrete evidence showing growth in student engagement and formative assessment results. Impressed, the superintendent later turned to the principal and said, "You've got a strong instructional leader here. He's already operating like a principal."

That moment elevated the assistant principal's reputation in the eyes of his superintendent. He wasn't just the assistant principal who managed discipline; he was now viewed as a leader who could speak with authority about instruction, strategy, and results, and he did all of this in front of the superintendent.

You never know when your moment to pull up a seat to the big table will come, so you must always be prepared. The table was brought to the assistant principal's school, and he wasted no time unfolding his chair and pulling up to that table to show his instructional skill set. The assistant principal didn't plan to be the one answering the superintendent's questions, but because he knew his work, he spoke confidently about instruction and had evidence to back it up. He turned a simple district walkthrough into a leadership opportunity that put him in the spotlight in front of the main decision-maker in his district.

You never know when your superintendent will look to you for answers, so your preparation has to be constant. The way you carry yourself when the spotlight suddenly shifts your way can either cement your reputation as principal-ready or keep you boxed into the assistant role. Your seat at the table isn't given. It's taken by being ready every single time.

Here are three strategies to help you be prepared to pull up a seat at the table:

Strategy #1:

Always be ready for your "spotlight moment." You never know when your superintendent or district leaders will see you in action. It could be in a meeting, a walkthrough, or even a casual visit. It could possibly be at a sporting event. Regardless, it's crucial that you treat every space like it could become your interview. The assistant principals in these stories elevated their reputations, not because they planned the spotlight, but because they were already prepared. Build the habit of knowing your work deeply, being able to talk through your results, and showing that you think like a principal.

Strategy #2:

Speak up with confidence at the right moment. Having a seat isn't about dominating the conversation; it's about knowing when to step forward. Both assistant principals looked for the right opening, and then they used their moment wisely. They didn't ramble or share generalities; they spoke with clarity and conviction about instructional leadership. For assistant principals, the lesson is to be intentional, wait for the right window, then lead with confidence when it arrives.

Strategy #3:

Align your voice to the vision. When you speak up, it is important that you make sure what you share connects back to your school's or district's vision. The assistant principals in these stories didn't just talk about random successes. They framed their contributions around improving instruction and student outcomes, which were the priorities of the meeting and the superintendent. When assistant principals align their voice to the larger vision, they're heard and remembered as leaders who can advance district goals, not just manage tasks in their own building.

CHAPTER 8

Your Voice
Within the Vision

"If you want to lift yourself up, lift up someone else."
—Booker T. Washington

There was a dean of students who had been promoted to assistant principal. Her principal was new to the school also. She served in a middle school and was transferred to an elementary school. To make matters more challenging, the school had lost several veteran teachers over the summer that left the new principal with 16 vacancies. Some were filled with long-term substitutes, and other times, staff had to cover in rotations. To make matters even more challenging, discipline was at an all-time high, and the weight of it all was overwhelming the principal. The assistant principal wanted to support her principal's vision, which was supporting staff, so students could thrive, but she also wanted to contribute in a way that reflected her own leadership strengths.

Instead of stepping back or simply echoing her principal's words, the assistant principal saw a gap she could fill. Many of the new teachers were floundering. They either were fresh out of college, or they had come into the field of education from another field. They were desperate for support. While the district provided a monthly meeting for beginning teachers, the assistant principal proposed creating their own school-based new teacher program.

She presented the idea to her principal as a way to advance the school's vision. The program would include biweekly check-ins, opportunities for peer collaboration, and targeted sessions on the specific challenges of their building's culture and climate. The assistant principal even identified teachers with strong classroom management to come to and lead sessions, which built not only leadership capacity, but trust. She even shared with her principal that she was a trainer for restorative practices, which was another intervention that could be used to support new and veteran teachers. The principal, relieved to see her AP step forward with a solution, gave her the green light.

Within weeks, the beginning teacher program began to take root. New teachers felt more supported. Classroom management improved, and substitute teachers started feeling part of the team rather than placeholders.

Supporting your principal doesn't mean silencing your own leadership voice. The assistant principal aligned herself with her principal's vision of supporting staff, so students could thrive, but she did it in a way that leveraged her own strengths.

This is the key. Alignment isn't about repeating your principal's words. It's about amplifying the vision through your own leadership identity. Every gap you notice is an opportunity. Do you step back and wait for direction, or do you step forward with a solution that makes the vision stronger? When you choose the latter, you not only reinforce your principal's credibility, but you also position yourself as a leader who is principal-ready.

Visit www.myappath.com/Vision-Alignment-Worksheet to access the Vision Alignment Worksheet to help you identify gaps and find your own leadership voice. By noticing a gap and proposing a beginning teacher program, she advanced the vision while also carving out her identity as a leader.

When I was serving as an assistant principal, my principal had set a clear vision: improving our school's overall academic growth by grounding instruction in a new framework for best teaching practices. She trained the staff, modeled expectations, and consistently reinforced her vision. I believed in what she was building, and I wanted to do my part to support it.

As I monitored data, I noticed that our seventh-grade English language arts scores lagged behind the other grade levels. At the same time, I was working on my doctorate, and I needed a topic to study. I saw an opportunity to both support my principal's vision and contribute in a way that reflected my own leadership strengths.

I approached my principal and proposed an after-school reading intervention program targeted specifically at struggling seventh-grade students. I presented the data I had tracked, explained how I would weave the framework's best practices into the program, and emphasized that this intervention would complement and not compete with her vision. She loved the idea and encouraged me to move forward.

Week after week, I worked closely with the students, embedding strategies that pushed them to think critically, read more deeply, and engage in meaningful discussions. By the end of the school year, the results spoke for themselves—the students in the intervention program showed significant growth in their reading scores.

My principal celebrated the success, not just because of the gains, but because I had found my voice within her vision. I didn't try to create a separate agenda. Instead, I propped up her leadership by making her vision stronger in practice and in results.

From this experience, I learned that supporting your principal's vision doesn't mean standing in the background and echoing their every word like a parrot. It means finding ways to make that vision stronger through your own leadership voice. By identifying a gap in seventh-grade reading and proposing an after-school intervention, I wasn't creating a separate agenda. I was showing that I understood the principal's priorities and could advance them in a practical, results-driven way.

When you take ownership of a piece of the vision, you're not only supporting your principal, but you're also proving that you can carry big-picture leadership yourself.

Here are three ways to find your voice within your principal's vision:

Strategy #1:

Identify gaps and fill them with solutions. Don't wait for your principal to assign you tasks. You have to be assertive and look for areas where the vision isn't fully reaching teachers or students, then step in with solutions. The assistant principal who created a beginning teacher program saw a clear gap—new teachers were unsupported. By filling that need, she strengthened her principal's vision of supporting staff, so students could thrive while also carving out her leadership lane.

Strategy #2:

Align your initiatives to the principal's vision. When you propose new ideas, make sure they complement rather than compete with the schoolwide vision. I launched the after-school reading intervention and grounded it in my principal's framework for best teaching practices. Because it advanced my principal's vision, my idea wasn't seen as separate work, but it was viewed as a powerful extension of it. Alignment builds trust and shows that you're a team player with leadership capacity.

Strategy #3:

Leverage your strengths to add value. Your unique skills, experiences, and expertise are tools to make the principal's vision stronger. Whether it's restorative practices, data analysis, or instructional strategies from your own teaching background, bring those strengths forward. By doing so, you show initiative, add credibility to the work, and demonstrate that you're not just echoing your principal; you're elevating the vision through your voice.

CHAPTER 9

From Numbers to Impact

"Numbers have an important story to tell. They rely on
you to give them a clear and convincing voice."
—Stephen Few

When I was an assistant principal, I reviewed walkthrough data and noticed a consistent pattern. The learning objectives were posted in almost every classroom, but they weren't being revisited during the lesson. Students often couldn't articulate what they were supposed to be learning. They were only able to tell what activity they were doing.

On the surface, the numbers from walkthroughs looked fine. The objectives were posted, but strategically, I knew this was a missed opportunity for student ownership of learning and for teachers to use the objective as a tool rather than something just for compliance. My principal had adopted a best teaching practices framework initiative, and using learning objectives as a tool for instruction was a part of the framework.

I met with the teachers and asked them what they did with the objectives besides writing them on the board. Many admitted they saw objectives as a compliance task rather than an instructional tool. That was the *why*.

I began working on the next step and strategically planned how I was going to change the mindsets of teachers from viewing the objective as something they had to do to something they could utilize as an instructional tool. I led a short PD session on how to make learning objectives living parts of the lesson. I modeled for teachers how to annotate their objectives by highlighting key vocabulary and even drawing pictures to help define key terms within the objective. I discussed referencing them at the start, revisiting them mid-lesson, and having students reflect on them at the end. I also provided sentence frames like, "Today I learned…" and modeled how teachers could use exit tickets aligned to the day's objectives.

To reinforce the shift, I used our district's walkthrough tracker. Instead of just marking "objective posted," I would note how objectives were being used during instruction. Over the next six weeks, walkthrough data showed steady growth in objective-driven teaching. More importantly, students began connecting their work to the actual learning goals.

By the end of the quarter, teachers shared that the practice helped them focus their instruction. I was able to take what looked like compliance numbers and turn them into impact on student learning. Visit www.myappath.com/Data-Reflection-Guide to access the Data Reflection Guide to help you look beyond surface-level numbers and uncover the narrative your data is telling.

Strategic leadership means looking beyond surface-level compliance. At first glance, it seemed that teachers were meeting expectations because objectives were posted, but the deeper question was, "Were objectives actually driving learning?" By asking why the numbers looked the way they did and then shaping the next steps, I was able to turn a compliance task into a lever for student ownership.

Data can either be a mirror or a map. If you stop at the surface level, it only reflects what's already there, such as objectives written on a board or test scores in a spreadsheet. However, if you push deeper, data becomes a map that points you toward solutions. The difference lies in how you interpret what you see. Do you accept numbers at face value, or do you ask the harder questions that reveal the story behind them? When you dig into the why and build systems around it, you move from being a manager of numbers to a leader of impact.

At a K–8 school, teacher retention had become a growing concern. In exit interviews, several teachers said they felt overwhelmed and unsupported, but the comments weren't specific enough to act on. The assistant principal decided to dig into the school's teacher survey data for clarity.

At first glance, the numbers looked decent, and most teachers rated school culture as satisfactory. The assistant principal looked deeper and noticed one troubling trend—the lowest-rated area across grade levels was professional learning opportunities.

That insight gave the assistant principal the why. Teachers weren't leaving just because of workload. They felt they weren't growing.

The assistant principal started working on next steps. She proposed creating teacher-led learning labs where staff could open their classrooms once a month to showcase a strategy that was working for them, whether it was integrating technology, building student engagement, or differentiating small groups. She built a schedule, paired teachers as co-facilitators, and attended sessions to give feedback and spotlight successes in staff meetings.

By the end of the semester, follow-up survey data showed an increase in teachers feeling they had meaningful opportunities to learn from each other. Even better, turnover the following year dropped.

The principal later said, "She didn't just look at survey numbers; she found the why and created a system that turned data into growth and retention."

From this story, I learned that strategic leadership requires looking beyond the surface of the data. On paper, the teacher survey results looked okay, but hidden in those numbers was a deeper truth; teachers didn't feel like they were growing. By asking *why* the numbers looked the way they did, the assistant principal uncovered the real problem and created a solution that not only supported teachers, but it also improved retention. When assistant principals use data to build systems that help teachers thrive, they strengthen culture and show they can lead strategically. That's what it means to move from numbers to impact.

Here are three strategies you can use to do this:

Strategy #1:

Look beyond the surface of the data. Don't stop at what the numbers say on paper. You have to dig deeper to uncover the story behind them. In the walkthrough story, objectives were posted, so the surface data looked fine. However, by asking questions and observing practice, the assistant principal discovered that objectives weren't being used as instructional tools. Strategic leaders always push beyond compliance data to find the "why."

Strategy #2:

Connect the "why" to a clear next step. Once you understand *why* the numbers look the way they do, chart the path forward. In the survey story, Mrs. Daniels realized teachers weren't leaving because of workload. They were leaving because they didn't feel like they were growing. She used that insight to create teacher-led learning labs. Numbers only become impactful when they're connected to actionable next steps.

Strategy #3:

Build systems that grow people, not just track numbers. Strategic leadership isn't about generating reports; it's about using data to design systems that build teacher and student capacity. The assistant principal with the learning objectives created a system of walkthrough feedback that shifted teachers' practice. The assistant principal with the survey created learning labs that strengthened the school's professional culture. Both examples show how data can build people and culture, not just fill spreadsheets.

Voices From the Path Strategic Leadership Interview

Name: LaShaunda Pankey

Title: Assistant Principal

District: Charlotte Mecklenburg Schools

1. What have you learned about the importance of thinking and acting strategically as an assistant principal?

Thinking and acting strategically as an assistant principal is vital for driving both short-term solutions and long-term school success. By prioritizing initiatives, analyzing data, and anticipating challenges, I can make decisions that truly improve student outcomes. It also means collaborating with teachers, staff, and the community to create a positive school culture. I've learned that a strategic approach helps turn daily tasks into meaningful steps toward lasting growth for both students and educators.

2. Share an example where you used data, planning, or systems to solve a schoolwide challenge.

At our school, chronic absenteeism was becoming a major challenge that affected both learning and school culture. I used attendance data to identify patterns, such as specific grade levels, days, and class periods with higher absences.

Working with teachers and support staff, we created a plan that included early interventions, parent outreach, and incentives for consistent attendance. We also implemented a system to track progress and provide extra support as needed. As a result, attendance improved, and teachers reported higher student engagement in classrooms. This experience showed me how using data, planning, and systems can effectively solve schoolwide challenges.

3. How do you keep yourself from getting stuck in the day-to-day and instead focus on long-term impact?

To stay focused on long-term impact, I prioritize tasks that align with the school's vision and delegate or streamline less critical duties. I also set aside time regularly to reflect and plan for initiatives like curriculum improvements, professional development, and school culture projects.

Using tools like data dashboards and goal-setting frameworks helps me track progress and stay focused on the bigger picture. This approach ensures that my daily actions support lasting, meaningful change rather than just reacting to urgent tasks.

4. What advice would you give other assistant principals about showing they can "see the whole board" and lead strategically?

My advice to other assistant principals about "seeing the whole board" and leading strategically is to always balance immediate needs with long-term goals. Start by clearly understanding your school's vision, priorities, and data trends, so every decision you make supports the bigger picture. Build strong relationships with teachers, staff, students, and families, because strategic leadership isn't just about plans; it's about people who implement and sustain them. Use systems, data, and regular reflection to track progress and anticipate challenges before they become problems. Finally, don't be afraid to delegate and empower others; strategic leaders multiply their impact by creating a team that shares the vision and takes ownership of schoolwide initiatives.

5. **How has working with Dr. Mills helped you grow as a strategic leader?**

Working with Dr. Mills has been instrumental in helping me grow as a strategic leader. Dr. Mills models how to balance day-to-day responsibilities with long-term planning, showing me how to prioritize initiatives that align with the school's vision. Through our conversations, I've learned how to analyze data more effectively, anticipate challenges, and implement systems that support both students and staff. Dr. Mills also emphasizes the importance of collaboration and communication. By observing and discussing her approach, I've learned how to build strong relationships, empower teachers, and create a culture of shared ownership. Her guidance has helped me move from reacting to daily problems to leading with intentionality, ensuring that my actions contribute to meaningful, lasting schoolwide impact.

CHAPTER 10

Building Your Leadership Muscles

"Small disciplines repeated with consistency every day
lead to great achievements
gained slowly over time."
—John Maxwell

When I was a younger assistant principal, I treated walkthroughs like a compliance workout. My goal was just to "get the reps in" by doing as many as possible and checking whether objectives were posted on the board. On paper, it looked like I was doing the job, but in reality, I wasn't building any real leadership strength. Teachers weren't improving. Students weren't benefiting, and I was just burning energy without gaining muscle. Teachers began to take walkthroughs as a joke, and they even said I was simply doing drive-bys.

The turning point came when I realized that if I wanted to grow into the leader my teachers and students needed, I had to push beyond surface-level walkthroughs. Building leadership muscles meant moving into the discomfort zone by joining PLCs, unpacking standards with teachers, and shifting from vague, safe feedback to feedback that was clear, specific, and actionable.

At first, it was like starting a new workout routine. It felt uncomfortable to dig into content I hadn't taught or give teachers feedback that went deeper than "Great job" or "I didn't like that." However, just like with physical exercise, the more I practiced, the stronger I got. I learned how to ground feedback in evidence and standards, like saying, "When you used turn-and-talk, 80% of students participated. To boost engagement even more, try adding a quick written reflection before sharing." That kind of feedback actually helped teachers improve.

The results were noticeable. Teachers became more confident. They started inviting me into their classrooms, and they began seeking my input as a thought partner. My instructional leadership muscles were growing because I wasn't just counting reps. I was lifting real weight.

That's when I understood that leadership isn't built on compliance checklists. It's built on consistent, intentional work that strengthens your ability to coach, analyze, and partner with teachers. Visit www.myappath.com/The-Leadership-Muscle-Workout-Plan to access the Leadership Muscle Workout Plan that provides practical strategies for growing your cultural, strategic, and instructional muscles. Every walkthrough, every PLC conversation, and every piece of meaningful feedback is a rep in the gym of leadership. The more you do it with focus, the stronger you become. For me, that meant moving from surface-level walkthroughs to really digging into instruction, learning the standards, and giving teachers meaningful feedback that helped them grow.

Building your leadership muscles doesn't stop at instructional moves. Just like in the gym where you can't only work one muscle group if you want balance and strength, leadership requires exercising multiple areas at once. Once you begin to grow stronger in instructional practice, you also have to build your cultural muscles—the habits that create trust, connection, and resilience in your staff. Without those, your leadership can look strong on paper, but it can still collapse under pressure.

An assistant principal who worked at a Title I elementary school quickly realized morale among teachers was low. Teachers started the year strong in August. Their fire began to fizzle out in September, and by October, teacher morale had hit an all-time low. The teachers were frustrated. Many felt unseen, overworked, and disconnected from leadership. The assistant principal wasn't sure how to fix it, so at first, she stuck to the basics. She handled discipline, sent reminder emails, and covered classrooms when needed because although this didn't fix the problem, the teachers appreciated her for doing these things.

However, she soon realized that her actions weren't building trust or culture. Teachers respected her work ethic, but they didn't see her as someone who truly understood them.

The assistant principal decided she had to build her relationship muscles. She committed to spending 15 minutes a day doing what she called culture walks. She popped into classrooms, not to do instruct-tional walkthroughs, but to notice and affirm something teachers were doing well. She also began hosting informal coffee and conversations twice a month where teachers could share challenges and ideas in a safe space.

At first, it felt uncomfortable. Some teachers were skeptical, and word spread quickly that she was coming into their classrooms. They wondered if she was just checking another leadership box or spying on them, but she stayed consistent. Over time, teachers began to open up, share more honestly, and even suggest new ways the school could celebrate student success.

By the end of the year, the teachers' working conditions survey showed that staff felt valued by leadership. Teachers began saying things like, "They see us," and "I feel supported."

The assistant principal realized that building leadership muscles isn't just about instructional strategies or data. It's also about practicing intentional relationship building until it becomes a natural strength.

I learned that cultural leadership, like instructional leadership, requires consistent practice to grow stronger. At first, building relationships may feel awkward or forced, but when you keep showing up with intentionality, you start to earn trust. Small, consistent actions add up to big results. Fifteen minutes a day of noticing teachers' efforts or creating space for them to be heard can shift the entire culture of a school. That's the power of building relationship muscles; leaders become stronger. Staff feel supported, and the school community thrives.

Here are three ways you can build your leadership muscles:

Strategy #1:

Trade reps for results. Walkthroughs and leadership tasks aren't about the number you complete; they're about the quality of the impact. Instead of just "getting reps in," focus on giving specific, actionable feedback tied to standards and instructional practice. Your leadership muscles grow when you move past compliance and start adding real value for teachers and students.

Strategy #2:

Push into your discomfort zone. Growth doesn't happen in the safe zone. Whether it's joining PLCs, coaching in content areas outside your comfort, or having tough feedback conversations, lean into the discomfort. Just like building physical muscle requires resistance, building your leadership muscles requires you to consistently do the things that feel hardest at first.

Strategy #3:

Build consistency into relationships. Instructional strength means little without cultural strength. Commit to daily or weekly habits that intentionally connect you with teachers, like culture walks or informal conversations. Small, consistent actions compound over time, building trust and shaping school culture. Relationship muscles grow through repetition, not one-time gestures.

CHAPTER 11

Coaching with Confidence

"I think the most important thing about coaching is that you have to have a sense of confidence about what you're doing."
—Phil Jackson

I knew an assistant principal who had been at her school for many years. Principals came and left, but she remained a staple at her school, and she was a person whom all the teachers relied on. She was even friends with many of the teachers because they lived in the same community.

When observation season rolled around, she absolutely dreaded it, especially post-observation conferences. To avoid upsetting her friends, she simply checked the boxes: "objective posted"—check; "students were engaged"—check. The truth of the matter was, she didn't feel confident enough to coach teachers, especially her friends.

The teachers in the building who were her colleagues but not her friends began to talk. They felt she was not providing them with feedback that would help them grow (which, in turn, would help their students). During a grade level meeting with the principal of the school, a few of the teachers expressed their concern about the lack of feedback they received. They felt as though this was just another box for administrators to check off just to say it was done. The principal listened to the teachers and met with the assistant principal to share their comments.

The assistant principal knew she wasn't making an impact, but she lacked the confidence to have deeper coaching conversations with her friends. She feared that they would turn on her or push back with questions she was not able to answer, and then she would be exposed for not knowing the content.

The principal told her that she didn't have to know all the answers, but she needed to know what questions to ask to get them thinking.

Visit www.myappath.com/Coaching-Questions-Cheat-Sheet to access the Coaching Questions Cheat Sheet to equip you with coaching prompts to spark dialogue, reflection, and growth in every teacher conversation. She also shared benchmark data revealing that many of their students were not mastering priority standards that would be on the end-of-year state exam. She told the assistant principal that by not having coaching conversations with everyone, she was not only stifling the teachers' growth, but she was also hurting the students, which was evident in the data. The principal then shared examples of walkthroughs she had done and the feedback she provided.

The next week, the assistant principal took a new approach. She reviewed all the teachers' data, including her friends', and she wrote out specific questions tailored to each teacher about ways in which they could improve in order to increase mastery of priority standards. At first she was nervous, but surprisingly, all the teachers began collaborating and brainstorming together.

With every conversation, the assistant principal became more and more confident. She realized coaching wasn't about having all the answers. It was about partnering with teachers to find solutions together. Over time, the teachers in the building began to view her as a thought partner who was invested in their growth.

Your confidence in coaching won't come all at once. It will be built through the challenges you face. Sometimes, that challenge will be finding the courage to coach colleagues to whom you're close. Other times, it will mean holding your ground with a veteran teacher who pushes back or resists feedback. Both situations test your ability to balance empathy with accountability. Every coaching conversation you step into, whether easy or uncomfortable, is a chance to strengthen your leadership voice. The more you lean in, the more you'll see that confidence doesn't come from having all the answers. It comes from persistence, preparation, and practice.

Avoiding tough coaching conversations may feel easier in the moment, but it ultimately hurts both teachers and students. By staying in a compliance-based, check-the-box mindset, you aren't able to provide the kind of feedback that can help teachers grow. Confidence is built through practice, and real coaching happens when you partner with teachers in problem-solving.

When I was a younger assistant principal, I observed a veteran science teacher who had close to 30 years of experience. She believed that because of her experience, she was supposed to be marked distinguished in every rating category. Well, when I observed her, I did not give her all distinguished ratings. I knew when I met with her for the pre-conference, I would have to bring my armor—her data from benchmarks, EVAAS, and common assessments. Her students were not performing well.

After I observed her, I saw many areas where she needed to improve. She was not teaching the standard, which was a major concern, and she only had students working on handouts. She was livid that I had the audacity to not give her all distinguished marks. During her post-conference, I listened to her attentively. I shared her data with her, and she told me she did not accept what the data said because her students were learning. I then took a different approach and began to ask questions and give her suggestions on how to improve her ratings. Once she saw I wasn't going to back down, her guard came down, and she began to be appreciative. Before I even had a chance to follow up, she asked me to come and see how she'd implemented these suggestions. Over time, she became better, and her students started growing.

What I learned from this is that coaching takes both data and emotional intelligence. The teacher's resistance wasn't just about the feedback itself. It was tied up in pride, identity, and the fear of being challenged after years in the classroom. By listening first, sticking to the facts, and shifting from confrontation to collaboration, I was able to get past that defensiveness.

I also figured out that coaching with confidence isn't about overwhelming someone with data; it's about knowing when to push and when to pull back. By asking thoughtful questions and offering practical advice instead of just pointing out flaws, I turned a tough situation into a real chance for growth. Her change showed me that when coaching combines accountability with support, even the most resistant teachers can improve, and when they do, so do their students.

Coaching with confidence means blending data with empathy. It's about knowing when to challenge, when to listen, and how to support growth, even when you don't have all the answers.

Here are three strategies that will help you to coach with confidence:

Strategy #1:

Ask more than you tell. Instead of rushing to solutions, ask reflective questions like, "What stood out to you about student engagement during group work?" This helps teachers take ownership, think deeply, and build their confidence to improve without always waiting for you to fix things.

Strategy #2:

Let the evidence lead the conversation. Use student work, benchmark data, or walkthrough notes to ground the talk. This takes the heat off personal criticism, shifts focus to student outcomes, and helps teachers understand why change matters.

Strategy #3:

Balance support with challenge. Great coaching mixes empathy with accountability. Recognize strengths but also push teachers to stretch themselves with clear, measurable next steps. Knowing when to lean in and when to step back is what makes coaching effective and earns respect.

CHAPTER 12

From Feedback
to Follow-Up

"Follow up and follow through until the task is
completed, the prize is won."
—Brian Tracy

When I was an assistant principal, our zone superintendent would come out and do walkthroughs with me. After each classroom visit, we'd sit down and calibrate, making sure we were on the same page about what I'd seen. These walk-and-talks were a chance for me to build relationships with district leaders and show them I was serious about moving toward principalship. Being present, asking questions, and engaging in instructional conversations beyond my own school let me demonstrate that I wasn't just managing discipline; I was developing my instructional leadership. Of course, I always checked in with my principal first because transparency and alignment matter. With that support, these moments helped me get noticed and prove I had an instructional lens worth trusting.

After we finished our walkthroughs one day, the superintendent asked what my next steps would be. I said I planned to do another round of walkthroughs. She told me if I really wanted to move the needle on academic growth, I needed to follow up with teachers two or three days after giving feedback. Following-up creates accountability and builds your leadership muscles. It also helps teachers see you as more than a disciplinarian. She encouraged me to focus on growth feedback—specific, actionable, and grounded in evidence—rather than vague, subjective comments.

I learned that leadership isn't just about making observations or having conversations; it's about turning those into clear, timely actions through intentional follow-up. When you circle back, you show teachers that feedback isn't a formality; it's a commitment to their growth. Follow-up builds a culture where progress is tracked and celebrated, and expectations are understood as shared commitments to student success. It builds trust; teachers start to see you as a partner walking alongside them, not just someone hovering to criticize. Without following-up, feedback just becomes noise. With it, you strengthen your credibility, shift the culture, and establish yourself as a true leader of instruction and learning.

You need to know that feedback without following-up is wasted leadership energy. It's not enough to leave a note on a walkthrough form or make a quick comment in passing. If you want teachers to grow and if you want to be seen as more than a compliance checker then you must circle back. That's where credibility is built. Teachers will only take your feedback seriously if they see you show up again, reinforce progress, and help them sustain new habits. Every follow-up conversation you have is a chance to prove you're not just checking boxes; you're building capacity and showing that you lead like a principal.

Later, I observed an eighth-grade math classroom. I walked in at the beginning of the class, and the students were working on a warm-up assignment. Five minutes passed by, and students were still working on the warm-up assignment. While the students were working, the teacher was at her desk on the computer. Five minutes then turned into fifteen minutes. Some students were still working on the warm-up assignment, and others began to talk to their peers. Before I knew it, 15 minutes turned into 35 minutes. Students became restless. The noise level in the classroom increased. Students started wandering around the classroom, sharpening their pencils, or going to the trashcan. Others started asking if they could use the restroom. Some had their heads down on their desks. The teacher then stood up from behind her desk and asked, "Is everyone finished?" She asked the students to pass their papers up, but she did not review the warm-up.

By the time she finally moved on, more than half the class period had been consumed by the warm-up. The standard for the day hadn't even been introduced. The teacher missed the window to grab her students' attention for the remainder of the class because she wasted 35 minutes on a warm-up assignment that she didn't even review.

I documented everything that I saw, but I knew that just writing "shorten your warm-up" on the feedback form wouldn't change anything. I asked the teacher to meet with me during her planning period, so we could discuss the walkthrough. I told her I noticed the warm-up lasted 35 minutes, which caused students to become disengaged, and it left only 55 minutes for new instruction. I asked her to explain to me the impact she thought this had on students mastering the content.

At first, the teacher admitted she used long warm-ups to keep students busy while she took care of managerial tasks such as taking attendance and checking her emails. Then, she realized that by focusing on the warm-up for an extended amount of time and not engaging with the students, she was not having an impact on student learning. I listened attentively and told her that warm-ups were meant to activate prior knowledge and not take over the lesson. I suggested that we work together to design five-minute to seven-minute warm-ups that connected directly to the day's standard. Together, we created short, focused warm-ups with clear transitions into the lesson and strategies like timers to keep things on track.

I told the teacher I was going to do a follow-up walkthrough to monitor her progress and ensure that she was maximizing all of her instructional time. I intentionally followed up two days later and sat in during the first 15 minutes of class. This time, the warm-up was concise, and it lasted no longer than five minutes. The teacher quickly reviewed the warm-up and used the data to adjust the day's lesson. The transition was smooth, and students were actively engaged in problem-solving.

After class, I praised the teacher for shortening her warm-up. I explained that the shift gave students time to practice the core skill. The teacher smiled and admitted she felt more in control of the lesson.

Over the next month, I continued to drop in and provide feedback to reinforce the new habit, so that she would not fall back into her old way of doing things. Soon, the teacher's pacing improved, and student engagement rose.

Providing feedback without following-up rarely leads to change.

Visit www.myappath.com/Follow-Up-Conversation-Guide to access the Follow-Up Conversation Guide that gives you step-by-step prompts to use to turn feedback into sustainable teacher growth. If I had only written "shorten your warm-up" on the walkthrough form, nothing would have changed. She would have gone right back to her old habits. It was the coaching conversation, paired with specific strategies and a planned follow-up visit, that helped the teacher change her practice. Coaching is not just giving advice. It is walking alongside teachers until growth becomes sustainable.

Here are three strategies to help you go from follow-up to feedback:

Strategy #1:

Schedule your follow-up before you leave the classroom. Don't wait until later to figure it out. At the end of your walkthrough or feedback talk, set a clear time to check back in—whether that's a quick 10-minute coaching chat, a return visit during a similar lesson, or a PLC discussion. When you schedule a follow-up, it shows you're serious, and it creates accountability for both of you.

Strategy #2:

Anchor feedback in data and standards. Move past vague comments like "work on engagement" and connect your feedback to what the data reveals. If benchmark data shows students struggling with a key standard, tie your feedback to that. Then, follow up by checking how the teacher is addressing that standard in practice. This keeps conversations focused on what really matters for student growth.

Strategy #3:

Use growth-focused language. Teachers respond best when feedback feels supportive, not critical. Highlight progress with phrases like, "Last time I noticed… Now I see…" Take notes, so you can track growth over time. A follow-up should sound like a partnership working toward improvement, not an evaluation. That builds trust and credibility, and teachers will start taking your feedback seriously because they know you're invested in their growth.

Voices From the Path Instructional Leadership Interview

Name: Rebecca Pierce

Title: Assistant Principal

School District: Marion County Schools

1. **What do you see as the assistant principal's role in leading instruction at a school?**

Assistant principals must also be instructional leaders to make a difference in the school environment. The educational system is past the days of APs handling books, buses and discipline. Assistant principals should be in classrooms, attend PLCs, have data chats with teachers. They should make sure instruction is rigorous and includes high yield instructional strategies. They must analyze data to deter-mine strengths, weaknesses and opportunities for improvement, and it is their job to help teachers improve their instruction to improve learning outcomes for students. During the first few weeks of schools, assistant principals and principals should complete walkthroughs together to ensure they are calibrated and speaking the same language. Assistant principals should dedicate time to complete walkthroughs on their own and also play a role in evaluating teacher performance through pre-conferences, observations, post conferences and create plans of additional support if needed.

2. **Share a time when you made an impact on teacher practice or student results through coaching, feedback, or PLCs.**

Weekly, we have teachers submit their weekly assessment to me that is labeled with the Depth of Knowledge (DOK) level for each question asked. This ensures that assessments are in alignment to the types of questions they will see on their end of grade assessments. Teachers make predictions weekly to determine which students they think have mastered the content, students who may or may not have mastered the content (forming our bubble cusps groups), and students whom they are focused on getting growth out of rather than proficiency. We compare their predictions weekly with actual performance results. We also complete error analysis weekly to determine what classes performed the best to see if the content was taught differently by different teachers. This ensures we are utilizing data in real time to make adjustments for the following week and determine what standards can be utilized as spiral review rather than retaught whole group to allow us to keep up with current pacing guides and district mandates. We are also making an effort to make our hallways and PLC room more data driven. We are focusing on comparing students beginning-of-the-year diagnostics with historical standardized data to form intervention and enrichment groups. We should always know which students should absolutely pass and what students we need to focus on to help them grow and close academic gaps.

3. What was the most challenging part of stepping into instructional leadership, and how did you overcome it?

One of the biggest challenges for me at first was being younger than the majority of the staff members that I serve. Some of the staff in different locations had taught me when I was in school. The biggest ways to overcome any challenge in my educational experience is to build relationships, find ways to build capacity in your great teachers, and help teachers who are struggling either up or out. I also attribute my success in facing challenges by being a servant leader, I don't ask anything of our teachers that I am not willing to do myself. I also send feedback that is both positive (glows) and a few opportunities for improvement (grows). Another technique that has worked well in my experience is praising in public and reprimanding in private. The entire staff doesn't need to be fussed at when only a select few are not following directives that are required to do what is best for students.

4. **What advice would you give to APs who want to be seen as instructional leaders and not just managers?**

Make a weekly walkthrough schedule and try to stick to it. If are you able to allot at least 1-2 hours a day you can get in numerous classrooms and provide feedback. You have to make a concerted effort because all of the other responsibilities can get in the way. Once you start getting in classrooms and providing feedback, your staff will crave those interactions, and they will know that you are never in there as an "I gotcha," but you are there to help them grow and develop to do what is in the best interest for students. Also align your professional goals with the goals of the school. This will ensure you are getting in classrooms, getting in PLCs and having data conversations frequently.

5. **Why would you recommend Dr. Mills to assistant principals who want to sharpen their instructional leadership skills?**

Dr. Mills has a wealth of knowledge, and she is a true instructional leader. I learned how to be an instructional leader from her. She provides resources that are targeted to help schools, staff and students grow. She's worked in several different capacities, which allows her to help assistant principals grow in several areas to focus on the whole child. She doesn't take her job as a consultant lightly, and she will give you a mixture of tough love and support. She has a proven track record of growing schools and utilizing best practices to help students achieve academic success and growth.

CLOSING

Now that you have read this book, you carry the mindset, skills, and confidence to step beyond the role of assistant principal and position yourself as a principal-ready leader. Moving forward, you'll be equipped with practical strategies, a clear sense of direction, and the credibility to secure your principalship and lead a school with vision and impact.

The real transformation begins when you step out of theory and start implementing the strategies in your daily leadership. If you wait, you risk staying stuck in the cycle of handling discipline, experiencing doubt, and being overlooked while others move ahead into the principalship you're working toward. If you act now, you'll not only accelerate your growth and visibility, but you'll also feel the confidence, clarity, and authority of a leader who is fully prepared to step into your own school.

The following is a summary of the concepts that have been discussed in this book to help you become a confident and prepared principal:

Chapter 1: Wearing the Role Before It Fits: Learn how to embrace leadership opportunities before you feel fully prepared, so you can grow into the role.

Chapter 2: Second in Command, First in Mind: Learn how to lead with the mindset and decision-making of a principal, even without the title, to prepare yourself for future leadership.

Chapter 3: Be a Strong Number Two: Discover how to confidently step in when your principal is absent and keep the team moving forward.

Chapter 4: Leading the Culture You Want to See: Gain clarity on modeling the values and behaviors you want others to mirror within your school.

Chapter 5: The Culture Can't Rely on You: Recognize the importance of building sustainable systems that keep the culture strong without your constant presence.

Chapter 6: Two Cultures, One School: Learn strategies for uniting divided groups by aligning expectations and creating one cohesive identity.

Chapter 7: Have a Seat: Understand how to claim your place at critical decision-making tables and contribute strategically.

Chapter 8: Your Voice Within the Vision: Gain insight into how to support your principal's vision while amplifying it with your own leadership perspective.

Chapter 9: Building Systems and People with Data: Discover how to use data, not only to create effective systems, but also to empower teachers' growth.

Chapter 10: Building Your Leadership Muscles: Learn how consistent practice and feedback sharpen your skills for bigger principal-level challenges.

Chapter 11: Coaching with Confidence: Understand how to deliver coaching that balances clarity, courage, and support, so teachers trust your leadership.

Chapter 12: From Feedback to Follow-Up: Gain clarity on why following up builds accountability, credibility, and stronger instructional outcomes.

It's time to move from reflection to action. Don't wait for the perfect moment or someone else's permission. Start applying these strategies today and build the portfolio, confidence, and visibility that will set you apart. You already have what it takes to lead; this book has simply reminded you of the leader you were always meant to become.

NEXT STEPS

You have made it to the end of this book; that means you are serious about elevating to your next level. You are ready to move beyond the day-to-day grind of an assistant principalship and prepare yourself to get promoted to lead your own school. You now have strategies that go beyond discipline and compliance that will help you grow your culture, sharpen your strategic lens, and step up as an instructional leader.

I understand that we live in a microwave generation, and we want things instantly, but please understand that none of these strategies are meant to be quick fixes. You can't implement them all in a day, a week, or even a month. As a leader, you have to give yourself time to grow and develop. This can only happen through consistency, intentionality, and reflection. The more you put them into practice, the stronger you'll become.

Your challenge is to take the tools in this book and begin implementing them throughout the school year. Be strategic and analyze your school's data with a cultural, strategic, and instructional leadership mindset. Start small by choosing one big rock that you can take ownership of and make an impact. Stay committed to it and don't lose your momentum. As time moves on, begin to layer on other initiatives or projects where you can shine and show your leadership beyond the role of an assistant principal. When you do this with fidelity, your actions will both transform your school and catch the attention of the very people responsible for promoting you to the next level. Superintendents, executive directors, and principals notice impact, and your consistent, intentional leadership will make you stand out.

As you begin your journey toward the principalship, remember that you now have the tools to think like a winner, lead with impact, and get student results. Your path to promotion isn't about luck or waiting your turn. It's about you showing up every day and leading like the principal you aspire to be.

Congratulations. Your next level is waiting for you. Now go get it!

WORK WITH DR. BOBBIE MILLS

Through group coaching, professional development workshops, and leadership retreats, I help assistant principals and district teams build the leadership capacity needed for principalship.

Learn more at www.getelevatedvision.com

Ready to Elevate Your Leadership?

If you're ready to take your next step toward principalship, I'd love to work with you.

Whether it is through group coaching, professional development workshops, or leadership retreats, each experience is tailored to help you strengthen your mindset, sharpen your leadership skills, and position yourself for the next level of impact.

You've already proven you're committed to growth. Now, it's time to turn that preparation into promotion.

Presentation Topics

Leadership Mindset

Step Into the Role Before You Get the Title

Your mindset shapes how you lead before anyone ever calls you "principal." In this session, we focus on strengthening the internal foundation that drives visible leadership.

Attendees will learn how to:

1. Shift from assistant principal thinking to principal-level decision making
2. Project confidence and authority daily through communication, presence, and tone
3. Develop a growth mindset that sees challenges as opportunities for influence
4. Move from managing tasks to leading people and systems with focus and clarity
5. Align inner beliefs with outward actions, so others see you as principal-ready now

Cultural Leadership

Lead the Culture You Want to See

Culture doesn't build itself; it's modeled, shared, and sustained through consistent leadership. In this session, we uncover how to cultivate a climate in which teachers and students thrive even when you're not present.

Attendees will learn how to:

1. Model the tone and behavior you expect from your staff
2. Empower teachers and students to take ownership of the school's culture
3. Establish predictable systems and routines that reinforce shared values
4. Build trust and collaboration that turn expectations into lived reality
5. Use culture as a credibility builder that amplifies your leadership impact

Strategic Leadership

See the Whole Board, Then Make the Move

Strategic leaders think beyond the moment; they connect data, people, and systems to purpose. This session helps you build the clarity and intentionality to lead like a principal now.

Attendees will learn how to:
1. Analyze and interpret data to identify priorities that drive school improvement
2. Lead initiatives that align with the principal's vision and district goals
3. Translate data insights into actionable steps that create measurable impact
4. Prioritize time, teams, and systems to move the work forward
5. Demonstrate the strategic thinking principals look for in emerging leaders

Instructional Leadership

Coach Teachers. Build Capacity. Drive Results.

Instructional leadership is where credibility is earned. This session gives you the mindset and tools to lead teachers with confidence, communicate with clarity, and build a culture of continuous improvement.

Attendees will learn how to:
1. Build confidence in coaching teachers through reflective, collaborative conversations
2. Deliver actionable feedback grounded in evidence and student data
3. Use following-up to turn one-time coaching into sustained teacher growth
4. Connect teachers' practice to student outcomes and schoolwide goals
5. Strengthen instructional credibility as a leader who grows both people and results

ABOUT THE AUTHOR

Dr. Bobbie Mills is an educational consultant and leadership coach committed to helping assistant principals rise into the role of effective, impactful principals. With a career that began in the classroom, she has served as a teacher, assistant principal, principal, and district-level leader, giving her a comprehensive perspective on what it truly takes to lead schools with vision and impact.

Dr. Mills is the CEO and founder of Elevated Vision Educational Consulting, which is a company helping assistant principals develop the skill set to become confident, principal-ready leaders, so they can get a principalship promotion and lead their own school. Through her consulting practice, Dr. Mills founded *The Educational Elevator Program*, a professional learning experience designed to help 1st–5th year assistant principals, especially those in Title I and high-needs schools, bridge the gap between where they are and where they aspire to be. Her four-pillar approach—Leadership Mindset, Cultural Leadership, Strategic Leadership, Instructional Leadership—prepares assistant principals to think and act like principals before they officially hold the title.

Dr. Mills's mission is rooted in her own journey as a school leader who once felt unseen in the role of assistant principal. She now empowers others to claim visibility, complement their principal's vision while building their own, and lead through impact rather than position. Her driving belief is simple—no aspiring principal should feel invisible, and every assistant principal deserves the tools needed to rise, make an impact, and leave schools better than they found them.

Dr. Mills holds a Bachelor of Arts degree in Education from the University of South Carolina Upstate, a Master of Arts degree in Educational Leadership from Winthrop University, and a Doctorate in Educational Leadership from Nova Southeastern University.